THE·KIDS·CAN·PRESS
Jumbo Book of Gardening

Kids Can Press acknowledges the financial support of the Government of Canada, through the BPIDP, for our publishing activity.

Published in Canada by
Kids Can Press Ltd.
29 Birch Avenue
Toronto, ON M4V 1E2

Published in the U.S. by
Kids Can Press Ltd.
4500 Witmer Estates
Niagara Falls, NY 14305-1386

Edited by Linda Biesenthal
Designed by Karen Powers
Printed and bound in Canada by Kromar Printing Limited

CM PA 00 0 9 8 7 6 5 4 3 2 1

Canadian Cataloguing in Publication Data

Morris, Karyn
        The Kids Can Press jumbo book of gardening

(The Kids Can Press jumbo book series)
Includes index.
ISBN 1-55074-690-1

1. Gardening — Juvenile literature. I. Kurisu, Jane. II Title. III Series.

SB457.M67 2000   j635   C99-932820-4

Kids Can Press is a Nelvana company

Dedication

This book is dedicated to Miss Rumphius, the Lupine Lady, who continues to inspire both children and adults to do something to make the world more beautiful.

Acknowledgments

I want to thank Murray, Tyler and Curtis for all their moral support and years of hauling, digging and weeding. I am indebted to the children of Garden Avenue and Runnymede Public Schools and especially the children of High Park Alternative School, who shared with me the wonders of gardening. I also want to acknowledge the help of all those parents, teachers, maintenance staff and administrators who have worked with me on the school gardens. School and community gardening needs the commitment of many. I want to thank Chloe Swail for allowing me to use her bird garden plan as a resource in this book. Thanks, too, to Charles Kinsley, Terry Fahey and Kim Delaney for inspiring and helping me to keep on learning about plants. Thanks to Val Wyatt, who planted the seed for this book, Linda Biesenthal, who weeded and watered it, and Karen Powers, who created its wonderful design. Special thanks to Jane Kurisu for her accurate and humorous illustrations, which have added so much to the text.
— KM

THE·KIDS·CAN·PRESS

JUMBO

BOOK OF

Gardening

Written by Karyn Morris
Illustrated by Jane Kurisu

KIDS·CAN·PRESS

Contents

Introduction 6

HOW GARDENS GROW 8
A Plant's Life 10
Good Soil 12
Start Composting 14
A Good Place to Garden 16
A Bird's-Eye View 18
Picking Plants 20
Plant Labels and Seed Packets 22
Digging In 24
Sowing Seeds 26
Growing Seedlings 28
Planting Seedlings 30
Watering Your Garden 32
Weeding Your Garden 34
Gardening in Pots and Containers 36

FRUIT AND VEGETABLE GARDENS 38
What's That You're Eating? 40
Good Plants to Grow 44
Hills, Rows or Beds? 48
Seeds and Seedlings 50
Tending Your Patch 52
Pest Control 54
Harvesting Your Patch 56
Putting Your Garden to Bed 57
Saving Seeds 58
Three Sisters Garden 60

Giant Pumpkin Patch 64
Watermelon Patch 66
Tomato Patch 68
Salsa Garden 70
Mixed-Salad Basket 72
Scarecrow in Your Garden 74
Herbs for the Kitchen 76
Pole Bean Teepee 80
Sunflower Fort 82
Raspberries and Other Brambles 84
A Patch of Strawberries 86
Rhubarb Patch 88
Planting Potatoes 89
A Victory Garden 90

FLOWER GARDENS 92
Favorite Flowers 94
Planning and Designing 102
Beds, Borders and Baskets 105
Homegrown Bouquets 106
Sweet-Smelling Garden 108
Night-Blooming Garden 110
Everlasting Garden 112
Miniature Garden 114
Growing Grasses 115
Rock Garden 116
Shoe Full of Flowers 117
Hanging Garden 118
Garden of Old Roses 120
Special Gardens 122
Fairy Garden 124
Grandma's Garden 125

GARDENING WITH NATIVE PLANTS . . . 126
What's a Native Plant? 128
Why Grow Native Plants? 130
Native Plants in Danger 132
Native Plant Regions 134
Native Plant Profiles 136
Native Plant Communities 140
Native Plants for Your Garden 142
Imitating Nature 144
Planting Native Plants 146
Native Grassland Meadow 148
Native Woodland Garden 150
Collecting Seeds from the Wild 152
Native Wildflower Garden 154
Water-Saving Garden 156

WILDLIFE GARDENS 160
Creating a Wildlife Garden 162
Butterfly Gardens 166
Monarchs and Milkweed 176
Ladybug, Ladybug 178
Garden Bees 179
Gardens for Birds 180
Hummingbird Garden 190
Bluebird Garden 194
A Bird Thicket 198
Toad Garden 200

SCHOOL AND COMMUNITY GARDENS . . 204
Creating a Living Classroom 206
Getting Started 207
Designing a Schoolyard Garden 208
Time Lines for School Gardens 210
Schoolyard Peace Garden 214
Special-Needs Garden 216
Other School Garden Ideas 218
Community Gardens 222
Neighborhood Gardening . . . . , 226

PLANT LISTS 230
INDEX 236

Good Gardening!

This book is full of gardening plans and projects that will help you create your own garden. You can grow a Three Sisters Garden in your backyard or pots of tomatoes on your balcony. You can design a wildlife garden filled with native plants to attract birds, bees and butterflies. Or you and your schoolmates can join other kids around the world and create a Schoolyard Peace Garden.

This book is full of tips that will help you become a good gardener — no matter what kind of garden you grow. If you follow the four golden rules of gardening, you'll be a good gardener in no time. These golden rules come straight from the world's best gardener — Nature — and also from experienced gardeners who have grown green thumbs by growing good gardens.

✿ Start with good soil

Follow Nature's example and add lots of homemade compost to your garden soil. Cover your soil with fallen leaves and dead plants. This will attract lots of earthworms, and these pointy-headed diggers will work the organic matter into your soil. You'll end up with healthy garden soil, and you won't have to use chemical fertilizers.

❀ Grow plants that like your garden site

Plants thrive in places where they get the amount of sunlight, water and nutrients they need. Check out your garden site to find out how much sun and rain it gets. Then choose plants that match your garden's growing conditions. There are lots of sun-loving, shade-loving or drought-loving plants to choose from. Try some native plants that grow wild in your area.

❀ Fill your garden with Nature's creatures

You'll need bees to pollinate your plants and ladybugs, birds and toads to devour bad bugs that attack your plants. These creatures and others will come to your garden if you grow plants they like to eat. You'll end up with a better garden, and you'll be giving Nature a hand by feeding and sheltering lots of different wildlife.

❀ Create a garden that matches you

Grow plants that you like in the kind of garden you want to tend. Even in a small space you can create a garden that grows strawberries and sunflowers and that attracts toads, butterflies or hummingbirds. Be creative and have fun planning and designing a garden that's uniquely yours.

How Gardens Grow

Just like you, plants need a few essential things to grow strong and stay healthy. Plants growing in the wild get everything they need from Nature — air, sunlight, water and nutrients from good soil. In your garden, you'll have to give Nature a hand.

This section covers the basics of good gardening: how to start a garden from scratch in your backyard or on your balcony, how to make compost and take care of your soil, how to choose the right plants, how to plant seeds and grow seedlings and how to weed and water.

Get ready to garden!

A Plant's Life

All plants have one purpose in life — to produce seeds.
When they die, their leaves, stems and roots feed the soil
that feeds the next generation of plants.

When planted in warm, moist soil, a bean seed bursts its seed coat and develops roots. This sprouting process is called germination.

A small bean plant is called a seedling. Its roots anchor the plant and absorb water and nutrients from the soil.

Water and nutrients travel up the stem to the leaves. The leaves produce food for the whole plant. This food-making process is called photosynthesis.

As bees gather pollen, some pollen from the male part of the bean flower is brushed onto the female part. After the flower is pollinated and fertilized, new seeds begin to develop deep inside the flower.

The bean pods are the fruit of the bean plant. Inside are the seeds, and inside the seeds are tiny bean plants waiting to grow.

When the plant dies, dead plant parts decompose, adding nutrients and organic matter to the soil for the next generation of plants.

To find out how good your soil is, dig a shovelful from your backyard. How many earthworms do you see? If there's lots of worms, you've probably got good soil.

Earthworms are a gardener's best friend. They plow through soil with their pointy heads, loosening the soil so air and water can get to plant roots. They also eat decayed leaves and other organic matter and then excrete worm castings that are full of nutrients. All this plowing and eating mixes up the soil and breaks it into small pieces. Encourage earthworms to live in your soil by adding organic matter regularly.

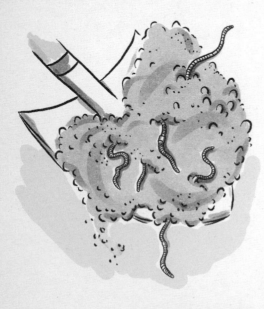

Good Soil

Good soil is full of dead plant and animal parts that have decayed (or decomposed), earthworms and tiny creatures called microorganisms. They are all part of the natural process that adds nutrients and organic matter to soil. If you have lots of nutrients from organic matter in your garden, your plants will grow strong and stay healthy. Organic matter also helps sandy soil hold water and clay soil drain better.

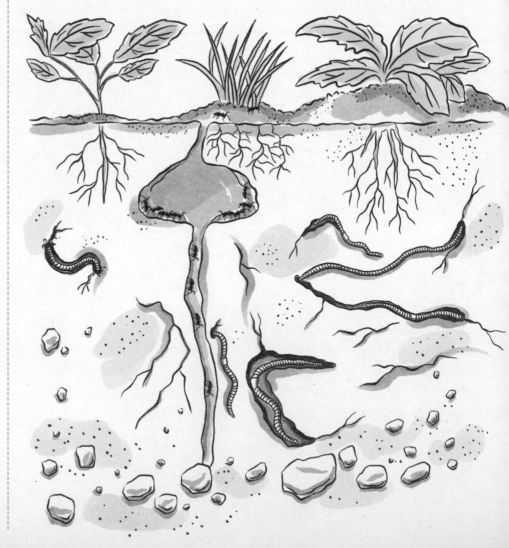

Organic matter in your garden

The best organic matter for your garden comes from compost you make yourself using kitchen and garden waste, such as grass clippings, egg shells, coffee grounds and banana peels (see p. 14). Here's how to use composted organic matter in your garden:

❀ If your garden hasn't been planted yet, spread 5 cm (2 in.) of organic matter on the surface of the soil and dig it into the top 30 cm (12 in.).

❀ If your garden is full of plants, add organic matter to the surface of the soil and let the earthworms dig it in for you. This method won't disturb delicate plant roots.

❀ Use organic matter when mulching your garden.

❀ In the fall, put a layer of leaves on your garden. They will decompose over the winter, adding nutrients to the soil.

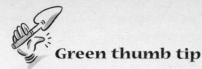

Green thumb tip

If you don't have enough homemade compost for your garden, use animal manure or peat moss that has been pre-soaked in water.

Mulch your garden

Mulch is any natural material added to the top of soil and around growing plants. It holds moisture in the soil, smothers weeds, keeps plant roots cool in the summer and warm in the winter. Try mulching with compost, grass clippings, leaves or wood chips. Add mulch in the spring when your soil has warmed up and in late fall. Mulch shouldn't touch the stems of your plants.

14 Brew some compost tea

Your plants will thrive if you give them some sips of compost tea. Put 250 mL (1 cup) of compost in a burlap bag or cheesecloth. Tie the bag shut with string, and hang the bag inside a pail filled with water. Let it steep for 1 week.

Start Composting

Organic matter decomposes slowly in Nature. You can speed up the process by using a composter. If you're gardening in containers on a balcony, you may want to buy a few bags of compost at a garden center.

Make your own composter

You can buy a composter at a garden store, but here's how to make your own using a garbage pail.

You'll need:
- large plastic garbage pail with lid
- utility knife
- hammer and large nail

1 With an adult's help, cut the bottom out of the garbage pail.

2 Using the hammer and nail, make three parallel circles of holes around the top, middle and bottom of the pail. The distance between the holes should be about 20 cm (8 in.).

3 Place your composter in a sunny spot, at least 30 cm (12 in.) away from any walls so that air can circulate around it.

Making compost

Layers are the key to successful composting.

1 Start with a layer of soil.

2 Add a layer of material that is fresh and green (vegetable scraps, fresh grass, weeds).

3 Add a layer of material that is dead, dry and brown (leaves, dry grass clippings).

4 Keep alternating brown and green layers. Each layer should be about 10 cm (4 in.) thick.

5 Keep the lid on your composter. Your compost is ready when it looks dark brown and smells like earth.

6 Don't add meat, fish bones, dairy products or kitty litter to your composter. They create a smelly mess and attract rodents and raccoons.

Lead alert!

If you're growing vegetables near a busy road or an industrial area, get your soil tested to find out if it has a high level of lead. Eating vegetables grown in soil with too much lead in it may cause lead poisoning. Your local department of agriculture office will tell you how to get your soil test done and help you understand the results. If the lead level in your soil is too high, plant your vegetables in containers filled with soil bought from a garden center.

A Good Place to Garden

If you're planning your first garden, start with a small one. All you need to grow some vegetables is a sunny spot that is 1 m (3 ft.) square. A flower bed that is 150 cm (4 ft.) long and 60 cm (2 ft.) wide will give you plenty of room to grow your favorite blooms. Pick the right plants and even your small garden will attract butterflies, toads and other wildlife.

If you don't have a yard to garden in, grow tomatoes or tulips or almost anything else in pots and containers on your balcony.

Good spots

🌼 Grow your garden in a sunny spot. Most of your favorite vegetables and flowers need 6 to 8 hours of sun a day.

🌼 Find a spot that is level so the rain doesn't wash the topsoil away.

🌼 Grow your garden close to a source of water and near your compost bin.

Bad spots

🌼 Don't grow your garden near a big tree. Its roots will steal nutrients and water from your garden plants.

🌼 Don't grow your garden beside a building that casts a big shadow.

🌼 Don't grow your garden where dogs run and kids play.

🌼 Don't grow your garden where puddles form after a heavy rain.

A Bird's-Eye View

Imagine you were a bird flying over the spot where you want to plant your garden. What would you see? Your house casting a big shadow in the afternoon? A wide open place that gets lots of sun all day?

Drawing a bird's-eye view of your garden will show you where everything is: sunny spots, shady spots, puddles, trees. This will help you pick the right plants for every spot in your garden.

Drawing a bird's-eye view

Here's how to draw a bird's-eye view of your garden.

You'll need:
- measuring tape
- ruler
- paper
- pencil
- compass

1 Measure the width and length of your garden site.

2 Choose a scale — such as 2 cm = 1 m or 1 in. = 1 ft. — to represent your garden on paper.

3 Draw your garden's size and shape to scale on the paper.

4 Using a compass, mark north, south, east and west on the paper.

5 Draw in any trees, shrubs, fences or buildings that are near your site. Try to draw them to scale.

6 Mark where your garden gets sun at 9 A.M., at noon and at 4 P.M.

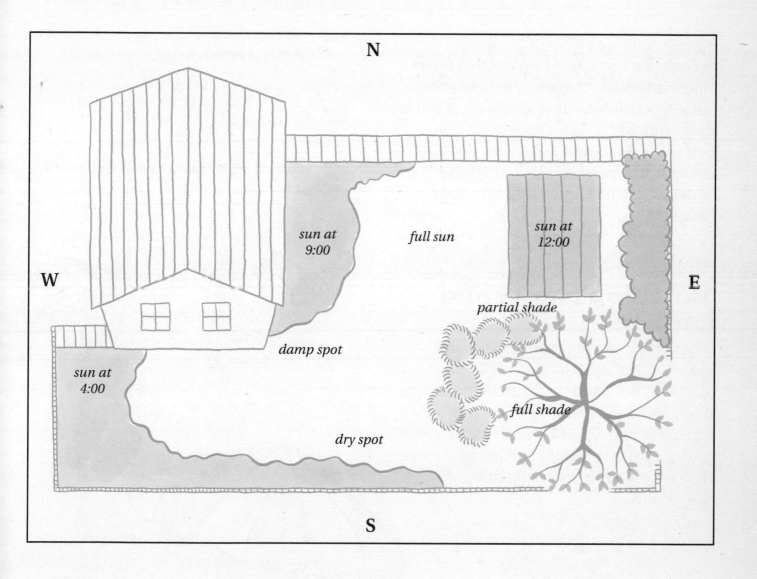

N

W   E

sun at 9:00   *full sun*   *sun at 12:00*

partial shade

damp spot

sun at 4:00

full shade

dry spot

S

7 Mark the spots that get full sun, partial sun and full shade.

8 Mark damp spots and dry spots.

Picking Plants

A sunflower won't grow in the shade of an old oak tree because it's a plant that needs lots of sun. So do tomatoes, potatoes and butterfly bushes. Lettuce likes a bit of sun in the morning and shade during the hottest part of the day. So do violets and lilies-of-the-valley. Ferns and hostas will thrive under an oak tree because they're shade-loving plants.

Matching plants and gardens

When choosing your plants, follow the golden rule of gardening — match your plants to your garden. Pick shade-lovers for shady spots and sun-lovers for sunny spots. You'll also have to pick plants that like your garden's growing season and hardiness zone. Here are the most important things you'll have to match.

❀ Sun and shade

Watch for full-sun, partial-sun and full-shade symbols on plant labels and seed packets and in plant and seed catalogs. They tell you how much sun and shade each plant likes best.

 This is a sun-loving plant that needs 6 hours of sun a day.

 This is a plant that needs some shade during the day.

 This is a plant that grows well in full shade.

✿ First frost, last frost

Some seeds can be sown and some plants planted before the last frost in the spring, but many won't survive even a nip of frost. To pick the right plants for your garden, you'll need to know the approximate date of the last frost in the spring and the first frost in the fall.

✿ Hardiness zones

The plants you pick have to be hardy enough to live in the climate you're gardening in. North America is divided into plant hardiness zones. Each zone has a number (sometimes followed by a letter).

Most plant labels carry the plant's hardiness zone number. The smaller the number, the colder the average temperatures and the hardier the plants have to be to survive. If you're gardening in zone 6b, you can grow plants from zones 6 and under. To find your garden's hardiness zone, ask at a local garden center or look at a hardiness zone map in a seed catalog.

Making plant checklists

Making a plant checklist for each plant that you like is a good way of making sure that it will grow in your garden.

Plant checklist:

Name of plant: _____

_____

Full-grown size: _____

Flower color: _____

Earliest planting date:

_____

Hardiness zone: _____

Perennial _____ /Annual _____

Full sun ___ / Part shade ___ /

Full shade ___

Soil: sand/ loam/ clay

Water: dry/ normal/ damp

Special features: _____

_____

_____

_____

Plant Labels and Seed Packets

Plant labels and seed packets tell you a lot about plants. Before buying a plant or seeds, read the label or packet carefully. It will tell you whether a plant needs full sun or shade, when to plant it and what hardiness zone to plant it in. Here's what you'll find on a typical plant label.

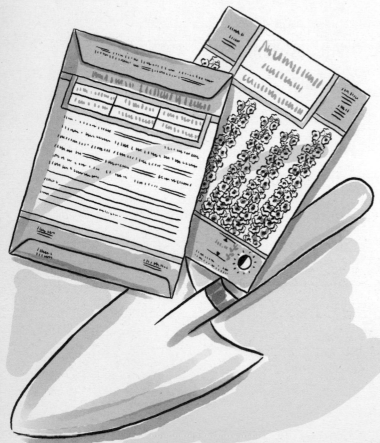

- **Botanical name:** Plants have Latin or Greek "scientific" names. The first part is the plant's genus (or group). The second part is its species (or kind). Each species has a different botanical name.

- **Variety:** Species of plants may have a number of varieties that produce different colors of flowers or plant sizes.

- **Common name:** This is a plant's nickname, which can be different from place to place.

- **Type of plant:** This indicates whether a plant is a tree, a shrub, an annual (a plant that blooms, produces seeds and dies in one season), a biennial (a plant that needs two growing seasons to bloom and produce seeds before it dies) or a perennial (a plant that blooms year after year).

- **Height:** A plant's full-grown height

- **Spread:** A plant's full-grown width

- **Spacing:** How far apart a plant needs to be from other plants

- **Location:** How much sun a plant needs

- **Flowering time:** When the plant usually blooms

- **Hardiness zone:** Which zones the plant will grow in

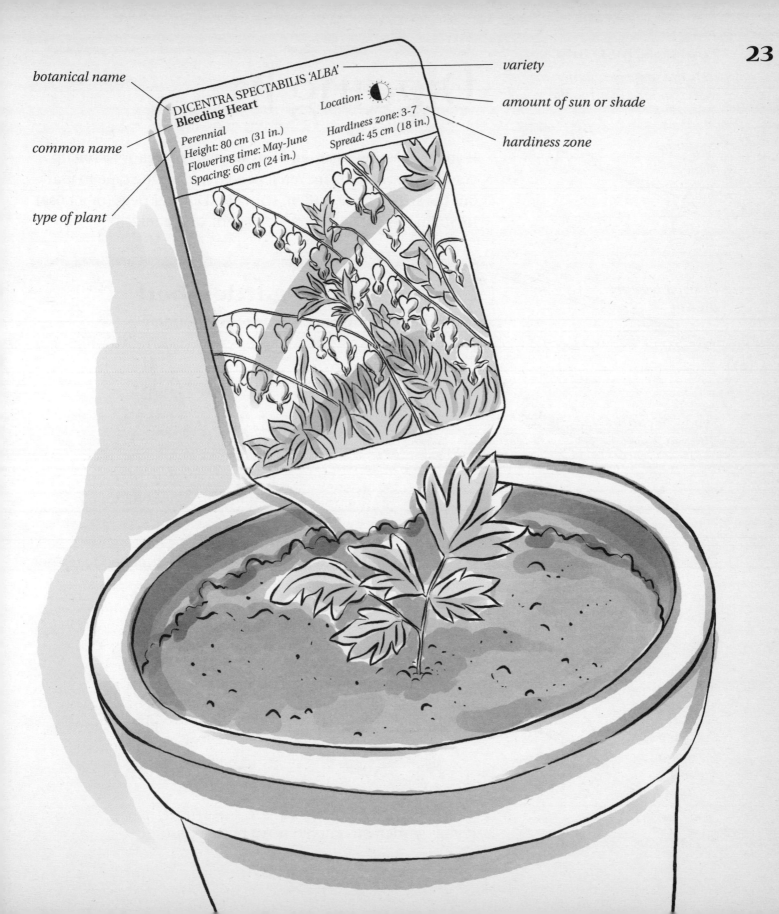

botanical name

common name

type of plant

variety

amount of sun or shade

hardiness zone

DICENTRA SPECTABILIS 'ALBA'
Bleeding Heart
Perennial
Height: 80 cm (31 in.)
Flowering time: May-June
Spacing: 60 cm (24 in.)

Location:

Hardiness zone: 3-7
Spread: 45 cm (18 in.)

24 Tools of the trade

Here are some gardening tools you may want to buy or borrow.

Shovel for digging

Rake for leveling the soil

Spade for cutting through grass

Hoe for breaking up clumps of soil and removing big weeds

Garden fork for loosening the soil

Digging In

If you're creating a garden from scratch, get ready to roll up your sleeves and dig in. You'll need a measuring tape to mark out the size of your garden, string and corner pegs (or a hose) to outline its shape, a shovel or spade and a rake.

From grass to garden bed

1 Outline the size and shape of your garden.

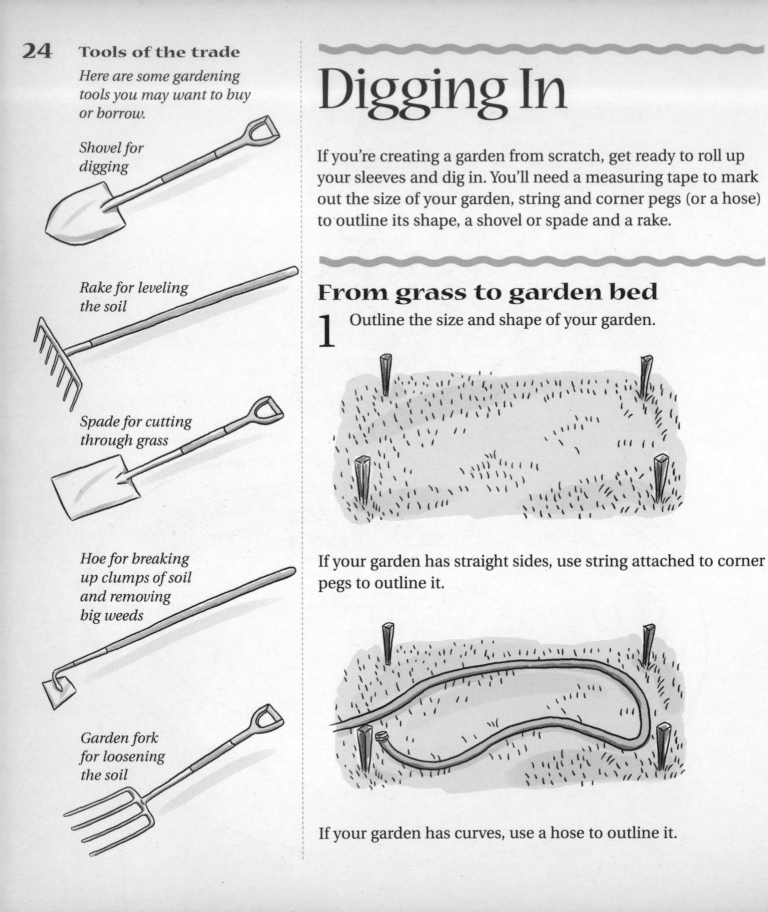

If your garden has straight sides, use string attached to corner pegs to outline it.

If your garden has curves, use a hose to outline it.

2 Using a spade or shovel, cut into the grass around the outline.

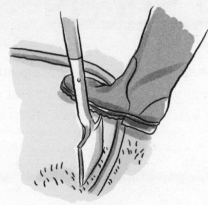

3 Cut the grass inside the garden into small sections.

4 Wedge the spade under each section of grass and lift it out, roots and all.

5 If your soil has big lumps, break them up with a hoe or spade.

6 Mix a 2.5 cm (1 in.) layer of compost into the top 30 cm (1 ft.) of soil.

7 Rake the top of the soil smooth before you begin to plant.

Green thumb tips

- *Plant seeds about two times deeper than their diameter.*

- *Very tiny seeds can be mixed with sand to make them easier to sprinkle on the soil.*

- *Put a label in your row or square so you'll know what you've planted.*

Sowing Seeds

You can buy seeds in the spring in garden centers and from seed catalogs. If you are ordering seeds from a seed catalog, order them early so you'll have all your seeds when you're ready to plant them.

When to sow

It's spring, but is it the right time to start planting your garden? Just squeeze a handful of soil to find out.

Take a handful of soil and squeeze it into a ball. Poke your finger into it. If it falls apart, it's time to plant. If it sticks together, wait a few days and try the squeeze test again. Your soil is ready for planting when it feels moist, but not soggy.

How to sow

Your seeds will be easier to plant if you choose a day when the soil is dry.

You'll need:
- rake
- seeds
- watering can with a rose nozzle

1 Rake the soil flat.

2 Rake the soil again using the rake upside down to make a small pile of soil on one side of your planting spot.

3 For small seeds, take a pinch of them between your fingers and sprinkle them on the soil, spreading them evenly so they don't clump together. Plant larger seeds one by one, leaving the right distance between them.

4 Take a handful of soil from the pile you raked to the side, and cover the seeds. Pat the soil lightly with your hands.

5 Water well with a fine spray from the watering can.

6 Water your seeds every day until the seedlings are 5 cm (2 in.) tall.

7 Thin the seedlings so each one has enough room to grow.

Growing Seedlings

Give flowers and vegetables a head start by growing small plants, called seedlings, to plant in your garden. Sow your seeds indoors about a month before you want to plant the seedlings outside. Seedlings need lots of light to grow — about 6 to 8 hours. If you don't have a really sunny window, use the special grow-lights found at gardening centers.

You'll need:
- soilless mix
- ¼ pail of water
- paper cups or peat pots
- spray bottle
- seeds
- plant labels
- trays
- plastic wrap

1 Add the soilless mix to the pail of water and let sit for 2 hours. Fill the cups with the soilless mix, leaving about 2.5 cm (1 in.) at the top. Press the surface lightly to get rid of air pockets.

2 Plant a few small seeds or one large seed in each cup. Press the seeds lightly into the surface and cover with soilless mix. Stick in a plant label.

3 Set the planted cups on a tray. Gently spray the planted seeds so the surface of the soilless mixture is completely damp.

4 Cover the tray with plastic wrap. The plant labels will hold the plastic wrap up.

5 Set the tray on top of the refrigerator. The heat from the refrigerator will speed up the sprouting. Do not set them in a sunny window.

6 Lift the plastic wrap for an hour every day. Spray well with water when the surface looks dry.

7 In a week or two, tiny green sprouts will appear. Remove the plastic wrap and set the tray in a sunny window. The temperature should be 15° to 20°C (60° to 70°F). Rotate the tray once a day. The seedlings on each side of the tray need their turn in the sun. Water when the surface looks dry.

8 When the seedlings are about 10 cm (4 in.) tall, they need to be "hardened off." This means getting them used to being outside. When there's no more danger of frost, place the seedlings outside for a few hours, in a spot away from full sun and out of the wind. Leave them out for a longer time each day. At the end of a week, they are ready for the garden.

Buying seedlings

• *A good place to buy healthy seedlings is from a nursery that grows its own.*

• *A healthy seedling shows lots of new growth.*

• *Don't buy plants that are tall and skinny ("leggy" plants), that have yellow or wilted leaves, or that have roots growing out the bottom of the pot (called "pot-bound" plants).*

Planting Seedlings

A good time to plant your seedlings is on a cloudy day, when the soil is wet and there is no wind. It's even better if there's rain in the forecast. Your seed packets and seedling or plant labels will give you information about planting dates.

You'll need:
• seedlings
• shovel or trowel
• compost

1 Remove the seedling by turning the pot upside down in your hand and then tapping the bottom of the pot. What you'll end up holding in your hand is called the "root ball." Set the seedling aside in a shady spot.

2 Dig a hole that is a bit longer and a bit wider than the root ball. Keep the soil you dig up. Put some compost in the bottom of the hole.

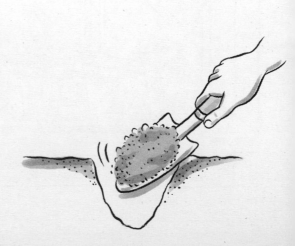

3 Gently set the root ball in the hole so that the top of the hole is at the same level on the plant's stem as the top of the soil was in the pot.

4 Fill the hole with a mixture of soil and compost.

5 Press the soil around the seedling firmly with your hands to get rid of any large air pockets.

6 Give your seedling lots of water after planting and for the first 2 weeks.

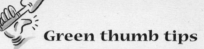

Green thumb tips

• *If your seedling is in a peat pot, you can plant peat pot and all in the soil. Tear off the rim of the pot and remove the bottom before setting pot and seedling in the soil.*

• *Trees, shrubs and perennials can be planted in early spring or early fall. Plant annuals in the spring after the last frost date.*

Green thumb tips

• *When planting your garden, put plants that like a lot of water beside each other.*

• *Conserve water by using a watering can with a rose nozzle, a rain barrel or a soaker hose. A sprinkler puts water into the air, where it quickly evaporates.*

Gauging your rainfall

Measure your weekly rainfall with a homemade rain gauge. Put a ruler inside a glass jar and put the jar in your garden. Leave it for a week. If the ruler measures less than 2.5 cm (1 in.) of rain, it's a week you need to water your plants.

Watering Your Garden

If too much rain falls on your garden, your plants may end up with waterlogged roots and some ugly diseases, such as gray mold and root rot. If your plants don't get enough rain, the leaves will wilt and soon the whole plant will droop. There's not much you can do when your plants get too much rain. It's a lot easier to save them when there's too little.

When to water

❀ Stick your finger in the soil. If it feels dry, it's time to get out the watering can.

❀ If your plant leaves are wilting, it's time to water.

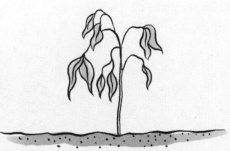

❀ Water your garden early in the morning. Nighttime watering sometimes causes plant diseases.

How to water

🌸 Water the soil, not the leaves.

🌸 Give the plant roots a good soaking so you won't have to water too often.

🌸 Use warm water if possible. Let tap water sit in the sun for an hour or two before watering your plants.

🌸 Build small water dams by making a moat around your plants.

Use a rain barrel

Using rainwater in your garden conserves water and is better for your plants. Rain is warmer than tap water and doesn't have chlorine in it. Set a rain barrel under a downspout so that the rain from your roof flows into the barrel. Buy one that has a lid and a faucet.

Use a soaker hose

A soaker hose lies on top of the soil. Small holes along the length of the hose allow water to trickle directly onto the soil. Snake a soaker hose through your garden so that it covers as much area as possible. Attach the hose to your tap and adjust the water.

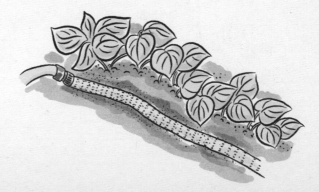

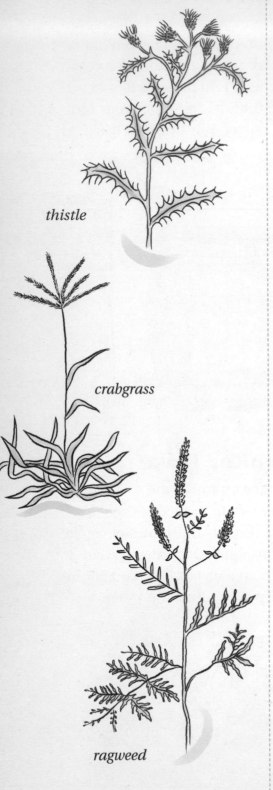

thistle

crabgrass

ragweed

Weeding Your Garden

A weed is a plant growing in a place where you don't want it to grow. Lawn grass is a weed if it's growing in a vegetable patch. So are seedlings from maple trees that poke up in your petunia bed. But don't forget that one person's weed — such as dandelion or milkweed — may be another person's favorite plant or some creature's food.

Bad weeds

Too many weeds, or plants growing where you don't want them to grow, will steal water and nutrients from your garden plants. Most common weeds are hardy and grow quickly, and will shade your sun-loving seedlings and slower growers. Here's how to control bad weeds.

✿ A good time to weed is soon after it rains. The soil is looser and the weeds are easy to pull.

✿ The best tool for weeding is your hand. Grab the weed stem and pull straight out. Try to get the whole root.

✿ For large weeds, use a trowel, hoe or garden fork to dig the plant out, roots and all.

✿ Weeds will grow quickly from seeds that fall on bare or disturbed soil. Cover bare spots with dead plants, dry grass or mulch.

✿ Don't use chemical weed killers called herbicides. They may kill worms and microorganisms living in the soil.

Potted plants

Here are a few tips for growing plants in containers.

• *Pots and planters on south-facing patios, rooftops or balconies usually need some shade. Grow a vine on a trellis to provide shade for plants and shelter for wildlife.*

• *Potted plants may need protection from strong winds.*

• *During the winter, empty pots should be turned upside down so that they won't crack.*

• *The larger the plant, the larger the pot it needs. Dwarf trees and shrubs need large containers, no smaller than 45 cm (18 in.) in diameter and 60 cm (2 ft.) deep. Half-barrels made of oak make good large containers.*

Gardening in Pots and Containers

Wherever you can hang a pot or set a planter, you can have a garden — and almost anything you can grow in a plot, you can grow in a pot. Put a strawberry pot on your patio or a basket of begonias on your balcony. Even if you garden in the ground, you can always add a potted plant here and there.

Barrels and old boots

You can buy containers in all sorts of shapes and sizes. There are clay and plastic pots, wooden boxes and barrels, and hanging baskets. But what will make your container garden unique (and cheap) are the odds and ends and recycled things you'll find at home to plant your plants in. Try some of these:

Preparing your pots

1 Place your container in its garden spot before adding soil, especially if it's heavy.

2 Place a piece of newspaper or stones over the drainage hole. If the container doesn't have a drainage hole or if it is very large, add a layer of stones in the bottom.

3 Fill the pot two-thirds full with pre-soaked soilless mix. Water thoroughly.

4 Sow seeds and plant seedlings. Add compost tea regularly.

Give your container garden extra height by placing pots on overturned pots, on ladders and on stairs. Hang more pots from hooks.

Fruit and Vegetable Gardens

Nothing beats a handful of peas or a bowlful of raspberries you've picked from your own garden. They taste better and they're healthier because you've grown them naturally.

If this is your first fruit and vegetable patch, start small — with just a few plants in your backyard or a few pots on your balcony. When it's harvest time, share your fresh-picked, home-grown crops with your friends, neighbors or a food bank.

What's That You're Eating?

If you love tomatoes, your favorite "vegetable" is the seed-filled fruit of the tomato plant. If you're a broccoli-lover, your favorite "vegetable" is the flower part of the broccoli plant. Knowing what part of the plant you're eating will tell you something about how to grow your favorite vegetables.

Cool-weather plants

If you're harvesting roots, stems, leaves or flowers, you can sow your seeds early in the spring when the weather is still cool.

✿ Eating roots

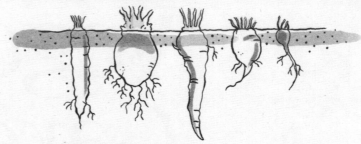

✿ Eating tubers (underground stems)

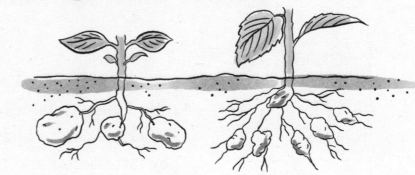

✿ Eating stems

❁ Eating leaves

❁ Eating flowers

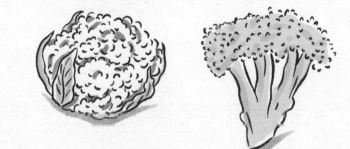

❁ Growing cool plants

• Leeks, onions, spinach and peas are called cold-weather crops and grow best in the cooler temperatures of early spring. Plant seeds outdoors about 4 weeks before the last spring frost.

• Carrots, lettuce, chives, parsley, potatoes, broccoli, cauliflower and cabbage are cool-weather crops. Plant them about 2 weeks before the last frost.

• In areas with warmer winters, cold- and cool-weather crops can be grown in fall and winter months.

• Most cold- and cool-weather plants grow well in a part of the garden that gets some shade.

Poisonous plants!

Whole plants and different parts of a plant can be poisonous. For example, you can eat a potato but not its vine (stem and leaves). Ask an adult before you eat any plant or part of a plant.

These are some plants and plant parts you should never eat:

buttercup
death-cap mushroom
mistletoe
nightshade
pokeweed
monkshood
yew leaves and seeds
foxglove
Jimsonweed
poison hemlock
privet
morning glory
bleeding heart
daffodil bulbs
holly berries
lily-of-the-valley
sweet pea
rhubarb leaves
fool's parsley
potato vines

42

Green thumb tip

After you harvest a cool-weather plant, plant a warm-season plant in the same place. Plant cucumbers after you've harvested your pea patch. Or harvest your lettuce early and then plant broccoli in the same spot. This is called succession planting. It makes good use of a small space and works well in a container garden.

No fruit, no feast

Fruits carry seeds and are produced after the plant's flowers are pollinated and fertilized. If you pick the flowers of tomatoes, eggplants, peppers, beans, peas, pumpkins, cucumbers or squash, no fruit will grow.

Warm-weather plants

If you're harvesting fruits and seeds, your plants need warm, frost-free temperatures for the seeds to germinate and the plants to grow fast enough to produce fruits and seeds before the first frost in the fall.

✿ Eating fruit

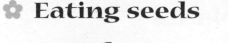

✿ Eating seeds

✿ Growing hot plants

• Sow your seeds after the last frost date in the spring when your garden soil feels warm to the touch. Warm-weather plants grow well in spots that get full sun, such as on the south and west sides of a garden.

• If spring comes late to your garden and you're left with only 3 or 4 months of warm weather, plant seedlings to give your tomatoes, peppers, eggplant and melons enough time to grow fruit.

• Lima beans, peanuts, okra and watermelon like hot weather and should be planted about 3 weeks after the last frost date. They grow well in southern areas where the summers are very hot.

Vegetables that need support

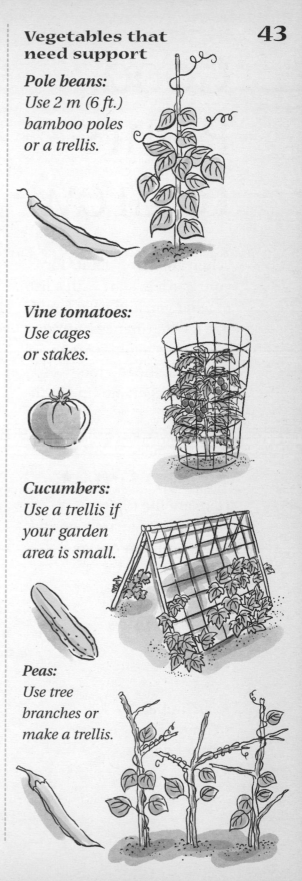

Pole beans:
Use 2 m (6 ft.) bamboo poles or a trellis.

Vine tomatoes:
Use cages or stakes.

Cucumbers:
Use a trellis if your garden area is small.

Peas:
Use tree branches or make a trellis.

Good Plants to Grow

When choosing plants for your garden, start with a list of what you and your family like to eat. Chances are your favorite vegetables are on the list of the top ten favorite vegetables in North America.

★ Top ten ★

Here are the top ten vegetables that are favorites to eat and easy to grow.

- Green onions
- Looseleaf lettuce
- Spring radishes
- Carrots
- Peas
- Beans
- Cucumbers
- Tomatoes
- Sweet peppers
- Corn

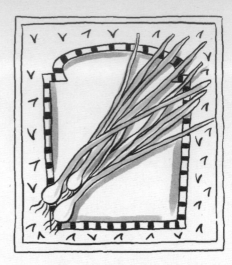

✿ Green onions

- Grow in a partly shaded spot.
- Plant seeds or sets (young bulbs) in early spring, 2 to 3 weeks before last frost.
- Water often.
- Bulbs sprout in 7 to 10 days.
- Begin harvesting when tops are 15 cm (6 in.) tall.
- Green onions or scallions can be harvested from any young onions before they form a bulb.

✿ Looseleaf lettuce

- Grow in a partly shaded spot.
- Sow seeds in early spring, 2 to 3 weeks before last frost.
- Keep soil moist.
- Seeds germinate quickly, in 7 to 10 days.
- Growing season: 40 to 50 days, depending on variety.
- Grow a variety of leaf shapes and colors to make interesting salads.

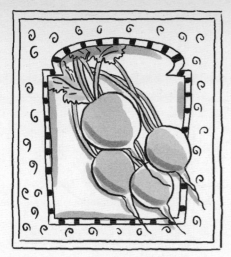

❀ Spring radishes

- Grow in a partly sunny, partly shady spot.
- Sow seeds in early spring, 2 to 3 weeks before last frost.
- Keep soil moist.
- Seeds germinate very quickly, in 3 to 10 days.
- Short growing season: 20 to 30 days, depending on variety.
- Plant seeds in cool weather for mild radishes and when it's warmer for hotter ones.

❀ Carrots

- Grow in a spot that gets morning sun.
- Sow seeds in early spring, 2 to 3 weeks before last frost.
- Keep soil moist.
- Seeds germinate slowly, in 10 to 21 days.
- Growing season: 2 to 3 months, depending on variety.
- Small and middle-sized carrots are easiest to grow.

❀ Peas

- Grow in a partly shaded spot.
- Sow seeds in early spring, 3 to 4 weeks before last frost.
- Seeds germinate in 7 to 10 days.
- Water well when plants are blooming and pods are growing.
- Growing season: 50 to 70 days, depending on variety.
- Snow peas are a very popular type of pea because you can eat the pods as well as the peas. There are dwarf plants that don't need support, but most peas need a trellis or fence to climb on.

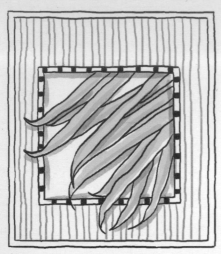

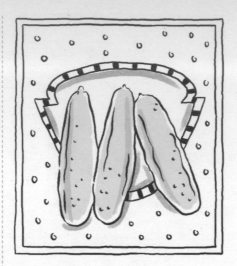

❀ Beans

- Grow in full sun.
- Sow seeds about 2 to 3 weeks after last frost.
- Seeds germinate in 7 to 14 days.
- Water the soil and roots, not the leaves.
- Growing season: 45 to 75 days, depending on variety.
- Beans grow as a bush (bush bean) or as a vine (pole bean) that needs support. There are string beans (snap beans), green beans, purple beans and yellow beans. There are also shell beans (lima, navy, kidney, mung, garbanzo and soya) that you can grow just for the bean seeds inside the pod.

❀ Cucumbers

- Grow in full sun.
- Each plant needs about 1 m sq. (9 sq. ft.) of space.
- Sow seeds 3 to 4 weeks after last frost.
- Seeds germinate in 7 to 10 days.
- Roots need weekly watering.
- Growing season: 50 to 70 days, depending on variety.
- There are cucumbers for slicing and pickling, seedless ones, sweet ones, ones with thin skins, tiny lemon-sized cucumbers and very long ones. Bush cucumbers take up less space and are good in containers.

❀ Tomatoes

- Grow in full sun.
- Plant seedlings 2 to 3 weeks after last frost.
- Add lots of compost.
- Use tomato cages or stakes for vine tomatoes.
- Roots need weekly watering.
- Growing season (from seedlings): 50 to 75 days, depending on variety.
- Bush tomatoes produce only one crop of tomatoes. Vine tomatoes need staking, but they produce tomatoes until frost. Cherry tomatoes are good for growing in containers.

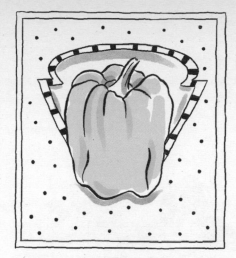

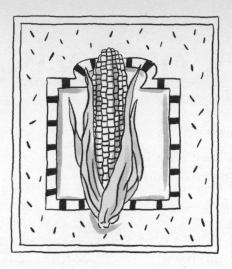

✿ Sweet peppers

- Grow in full sun.
- Plant seedlings 2 to 3 weeks after last frost.
- Add lots of compost.
- Roots need weekly watering.
- Growing season (from seedlings): 65 to 80 days, depending on variety.
- The sweetest peppers are bell peppers, whether they're yellow, red, brown or purple.

✿ Corn

- Grow in full sun.
- Plant seeds 2 to 3 weeks after last frost.
- Add lots of compost.
- Seeds germinate in 7 to 10 days.
- Roots need weekly watering.
- Growing season: 75 to 100 days, depending on variety.
- There's popcorn for popping, flint corn for grinding into cornmeal, sweet corn for corn on the cob, and Indian corn for harvest celebrations. In containers, try "baby corn" for tiny corn on tiny plants.

Vegetable checklist:

Use this plant checklist to plan your patch.

Name of plant: _____

_____

_____

Hardiness zone: _____

Cool ____ or warm ____ weather plant

Plant as seed ____ or seedling ____

Number of days to maturity.

_____

Planting date: _____

Harvesting date: _____

Needs trellis or stake?

Yes ____ No ____

Spacing:
How far apart in a row?

_____

Or how many per 30 cm (1 ft.) square?

_____

_____

Hills, Rows or Beds?

Arrow-straight rows aren't the only way to
grow plants in your garden. There are other,
and sometimes better, ways of planting your
plants.

❋ Rows

Grow your vegetables in rows if you have
a large garden. Rows make tending your
garden easy and give plants lots of sunlight,
air and room to grow. To get the most sun
for your plants, run your rows in a north to
south direction, and plant the tallest plants
at the back or side. Leave 30 cm (12 in.)
between rows. Mark out the rows with
stakes and string. If you have lots of space,
put wider paths between the rows, at least
60 cm (2 ft.), and pave your paths with straw
or newspapers (or another kind of mulch)
to keep weeds from growing.

❋ Wide rows

If you need to save space, try planting some
of your vegetables closer together in wider
rows. This is called "intensive" planting.
Carrots, lettuce, radishes, beans and peas
are some vegetables that won't mind a bit of
crowding. Wide rows can be any length and
are usually 30 cm (12 in.) wide. The seeds
are planted closer together than normal.

❧ Squares

This way of planting a garden makes good use of small spaces because plants grow close together. Try a plot that's 1 m (3 ft.) square. With a garden this size, it's easy to reach the soil and plants from all sides. If you want a larger garden, make several squares and put paths between them. Divide each square into 30 cm (12 in.) sections and plant a different vegetable in each one. When plants grow close together, their leaves keep the soil moist and the weeds from growing.

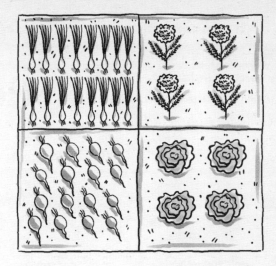

❧ Hills

Little mounds or hills are a good choice in a larger garden for growing vine crops that need warm soil, lots of compost and good drainage. Plant cucumbers, cantaloupe, pumpkins, squash, watermelons and zucchini in small compost hills that are 1 m (3 ft.) apart in all directions.

❧ Raised beds

These large mounds of soil and compost sit 15 to 30 cm (6 to 12 in.) above ground level. The soil warms up earlier in the spring for earlier planting. With such warm, compost-rich soil, you can plant your plants closer together and get all the benefits of planting in squares. To make a mound, mark out a rectangle or square with string and stakes. Rake the soil up from outside the mound into the center and add lots of compost. Rake the top smooth. You can also build a bottomless box and fill it with soil and compost.

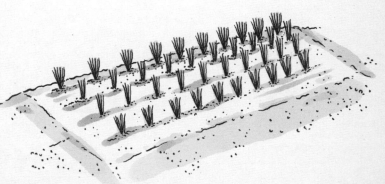

Put recycled milk cartons or juice cans, with bottoms removed, around seedlings to protect them from wind, bad weather and some insects.

Seeds and Seedlings

You can grow most of your vegetables from seed. The seed packets will tell you when to plant, how deep to plant, how long it will take your seeds to sprout, and how many days from seeding to harvesting.

Many gardeners plant seedlings (small plants) for tomatoes, peppers, melons, pumpkins and other crops that need lots of heat and lots of time to produce fruit and seeds. You can also plant seedlings rather than seeds just to get a head start on your growing season or on your neighborhood's first-tomato-of-the-summer competition.

Planting by the moon

Green thumb tip

Plant fast sprouters (such as radishes) with slow sprouters (such as carrots) to keep the soil loose and the row well marked.

Chemical alert!

Some seeds are chemically treated to prevent them from being attacked by a fungus before they've had a chance to push up through the soil. If your bean, corn and pea seeds are covered with a powder, handle them carefully. Keep them away from your mouth and nose. Better yet, buy untreated seeds (available in some seed catalogs).

One very old gardening tip says that some crops grow better when they are planted during the waxing phase of the moon (when it appears to be getting bigger), and other crops grow better if planted during the waning phase (when the moon appears to be getting smaller). Here's the tip: Plant underground crops — root crops (such as potatoes, carrots and turnips) — during the moon's waning phase. Plant crops that grow above the ground — leaf, stem, flower, fruit and seed crops (such as peas, beans and squash) — during the moon's waxing phase.

Tending Your Patch

Between planting and harvesting your garden, you'll need to spend only a few hours each week tending to five simple garden chores: feeding, mulching, watering, weeding and pest control.

❀ Feeding

Most fruits and vegetables need extra nutrients because they are annual plants and have to grow from seed to fruit in one season. Vegetables that produce fruit, such as tomatoes, peppers and melons, need lots of nutrients when they're blooming and the fruit is forming. Add compost to the soil around your plants or water the roots with compost tea every 2 to 3 weeks.

❀ Mulching

Mulch is a covering of leaves, grass or compost spread around the roots of plants to hold moisture in the soil and keep weeds from growing. Spread mulch around your seedlings when they are about 15 cm (6 in.), and mulch between rows to smother the weeds. Don't let the mulch touch the stems of the plants.

✿ Watering

Spray newly planted seeds daily with a fine mist. Water the roots of seedlings and plants — never the leaves — so they get a deep soaking. If you are using a hose, lay it on the ground so the water runs gently into the soil. During midsummer, most garden plants need about 2.5 cm (1 in.) of water a week.

✿ Weeding

Pull weeds at least once every three weeks. If you don't, your plants will be crowded out by weeds that block sunlight, steal nutrients and absorb water. It's often hard to tell which is new vegetable and which is new weed. Your plants are the ones that are all the same size with leaves that look the same. If in doubt, leave the weeding for another week. Add your weeds to your compost pile, or use them as mulch around your plants.

54 Make a snake

Many furry, four-footed garden pests will steer clear of your garden if it looks as if it's snake-infested. Use old pieces of garden hose to make your own snakes.

Pest Control

Don't let uninvited guests gobble up your crops. Try some of these natural, non-chemical ways of getting rid of the pests that are devouring your plants.

✿ Common pests

These are some of the most common garden pests and the plants they attack:

Mexican bean beetle (on bean leaf)

aphid (on a bud)

Japanese beetle (on potato plant)

tomato hornworm (on tomato leaf)

✿ Rotating crops

To confuse pests that spend winter underground in your garden, don't plant your plants in the same part of the garden each year.

✿ Hand-picking

Pick slugs, snails, cabbage worms, Mexican bean beetles, corn borers, Japanese beetles and tomato hornworms off your plants. Drown them in soapy water or step on them, and then add them to the compost pile.

✿ Magic potions

Mix crushed garlic and hot peppers, add water and spray this potion on the underside of leaves to kill aphids. You can also make a general bug spray using pure soap (not detergent) and water.

✿ Planting extra plants

Plan on losing some of your plants to pests or disease. Just plant a few more seeds. Native North Americans used to set out cracked corn in a spot far away from their crops to attract raccoons, squirrels, chipmunks, crows, pigeons and deer away from their vegetable plants.

✿ Companion plants

Confuse garden pests by planting several different kinds of plants together. The scents of the different plants get mixed up, and the insects can't find the plants that they like to eat.

• Plant dill near tomatoes to lure away the tomato hornworm.

• Plant onions beside carrots because their strong smell confuses the carrot fly.

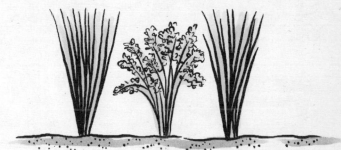

• Plant marigolds, mint, rue, tansy and sweet basil among your vegetables. They all have strong smells that many pests don't like.

• Plant nasturtium and lamb's quarters to attract aphids away from your crops. These are called "trap" plants.

✿ Good bugs

Attract good bugs — ladybugs, green lacewings, dragonflies and praying mantises — to eat the bad bugs by planting Queen Anne's lace, yarrow, goldenrod and asters.

Harvesting Your Patch

Pick most of your fruits and vegetables when they are younger rather than older, when they are sweet and juicy rather than tough and woody. The best way to figure out if your crops are ready to harvest is to pick a vegetable and taste it. Here are some other harvest tips.

✿ Hold the plant with one hand and pull off the vegetable with the other, trying not to yank the plant out of the ground. For some plants, such as squash and pumpkins, you may need scissors or a knife to cut the stems.

✿ Pick peas and beans before they completely fill out their pods or they will be too tough to eat.

✿ Zucchini and cucumbers are famous for growing from babies to behemoths when your back is turned, so it's best to start picking them when they are about 10 to 15 cm (4 to 6 in.) long.

✿ The more you pick, the more you get. Peas, beans and cucumbers will produce larger crops if picked often and regularly.

✿ Dig up root crops, such as carrots and potatoes, on cloudy days.

✿ Corn, beans and tomatoes are very sensitive to cold temperatures, so harvest them well before frost.

Putting Your Garden to Bed

An autumn frost will kill most of your annual plants. When their leaves wilt and turn dark and mushy, that's a sure sign their growing days are over. It's time to tuck your garden in for the winter.

✿ Dig your bean and pea plants into the soil. They will add nitrogen for next year's crops.

✿ Leave perennial plants in the garden or in pots outside. You may want to mark them so they don't accidentally get dug up or tossed out.

✿ Pull out your annual plants and either add them to the compost pile or dig them into the soil. They will break down over the winter.

✿ Diseased plants should be tossed into the garbage rather than in the compost pile.

✿ Add a layer of compost or dried leaves to your plots and pots, and dig it in.

✿ After harvesting vegetables grown in containers, empty the containers, wash them out and turn them over for the winter.

58

Green thumb tip

If you're harvesting leaves (lettuce) or roots (radishes), be sure to let a few plants "go to seed."

This lettuce plant has been left to produce seeds.

Saving Seeds

Vegetable seeds are easy to buy, but many good gardeners grow their own. To grow your own seeds, your plants have to flower and get pollinated so they produce the fruit that holds the seeds.

❀ Which seeds?

When your crops are up and growing well, choose a few plants that look healthy. Tie a string around their stems so you remember not to eat them. Let the plants produce fruit. Leave them in the garden until fall.

✿ Harvesting seeds

When the pods of beans and peas become dry, pick them before they burst and remove the seeds from the pods. Vegetables with fleshy fruit, such as tomatoes and squash, should be left to over-ripen on the plant (without rotting).

After harvesting your seeds, spread them out on a newspaper and let them dry for a few days. When the seeds are completely dry, store them in glass jars in a cool, dark place.

Three Sisters Garden

An old Iroquois story tells how Sky Woman, the creator of the world and everything in it, gave corn, beans and squash to the Iroquois people. The three vegetables were perfect companions. The corn stalks gave the beans a support to climb up. The roots of the beans added nitrogen to the soil to feed the corn and squash. The big, prickly leaves of the squash kept corn-loving raccoons away.

These three vegetables provided many Native North Americans with a healthy diet. The Iroquois name for the Three Sisters means "life support."

Plant the Three Sisters

You'll need:

- garden space about 3 m (9 ft.) square.
- 9 fish heads (from a fish market, or catch your own)
- compost
- packet of corn seeds
- packet of pole bean seeds
- packet of squash seeds
- compass
- compost tea

1 Mark out three rows that are about 3 m (about 9 ft.) long and 1 m (3 ft.) apart.

2 In each row, make three holes, each one 13 cm (5 in.) deep and 1 m (3 ft.) apart.

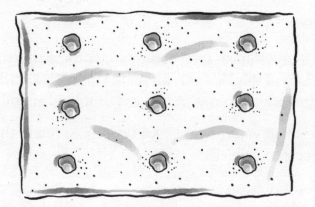

3 Put a fish head in each hole to fertilize the plants. Fill the rest of the hole with a mixture of soil and compost.

Green thumb tips

- *Try growing Native North American varieties of corn, such as 'Rainbow Inca', 'Black Aztec' and 'Hopi Pink', in your Three Sisters garden.*

- *To keep away corn borers, add a drop of mineral oil to the silk of each ear of corn when it begins to brown.*

Fish heads?

Corn and squash need lots of nitrogen to grow. The roots of the bean plants add some nitrogen to the soil, but fish heads add lots more. If you can't get fish heads, try using other natural fertilizers containing fish products.

62

Green thumb tip

If you plant more than one variety of corn and they cross-pollinate, you'll get mixed-up corn seeds.

4 On top of each hole, make a hill of soil and compost 45 cm. (18 in.) wide and 10 cm (4 in.) high. Make a moat on the top of each hill to hold water for thirsty corn.

5 Plant four corn seeds about 8 cm (3 in.) deep in the top of each hill so that each one faces a different direction, north, east, south and west (use a compass, or find your directions from the sun).

6 When the corn has grown finger-high, about 10 cm (4 in.), plant four pole or climbing bean seeds halfway down the hill, at each compass point.

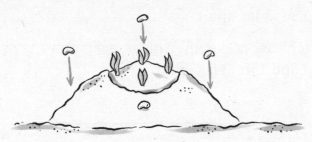

7 Plant one squash seed at the same time as the beans at the bottom of the hill. You can plant summer squash, such as zucchini, or winter squash, such as pumpkins or gourds.

8 Weed and water weekly. Add compost tea to the hills every 2 to 3 weeks.

9 When the bean plants grow longer, wrap them around the corn stalks.

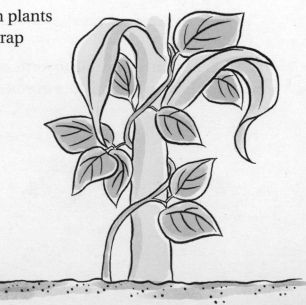

Harvesting the Three Sisters

❁ Corn

Harvest corn in the afternoon when the sugar level is highest. The corn is ready to pick when the tips of the silk on an ear of corn turns dry and brown, about 13 weeks after planting. Test a kernel of corn by breaking it open with your fingernail. If the juice is milky, it's time to pick. Bend the ears down and twist. Pick only what you need for each meal.

❁ Beans

Pick beans in about 8 weeks, when they are about 10 cm (4 in.) long and before the pods become lumpy. Pick beans every 2 to 3 days so more beans will grow. Don't pick beans when the leaves are wet.

❁ Summer squash

Harvest summer squash, such as zucchini, in about 8 weeks, when they are about 15 cm (6 in.) long. Cut them off at the stem.

❁ Winter squash

Harvest winter squash at first frost. When the skin of the squash is hard, cut the stalk with a knife or scissors. Leave 10 cm (4 in.) of stem attached to keep the squash from rotting. Let squash sit for a week in the sun to toughen the skin. Store winter squash in a cool, dry room. Pumpkins are ready to harvest when they turn orange, about 12 weeks after planting.

The story of the Three Sisters

Long ago three sisters lived together in a sunny field. The oldest was very tall. She had long, yellow hair and wore a green shawl. The second sister was dressed in green. At first she crawled along the ground and then wrapped herself around her older sister. The third sister wore a yellow dress and ran wild, all over her sisters' feet. In late summer, a girl came to visit them. That night the second sister dressed in green disappeared. A few weeks later the girl came again. That night the sister in the yellow dress disappeared. The oldest sister was sad and lonely without the company of her two younger sisters. Her green shawl faded and her hair tangled in the wind. When the nights had grown cold, the girl returned to the field. She took the oldest sister in her arms and carried her home to the longhouse. There the oldest sister found her two sisters helping the girl's family prepare and store food for the long winter ahead. She offered to help by grinding corn for the family. The three sisters promised they would never be separated again.

Personal pumpkins

Carve your name or initials with a nail into the skin of a young pumpkin. Watch the letters grow as the pumpkin does.

Giant Pumpkin Patch

Pumpkins belong to the same vegetable family as squash, cucumbers, cantaloupe or muskmelon and watermelon. Their growing seasons may be different, but their growing conditions are the same — full sun, weekly watering and lots of compost.

To grow really, really big pumpkins, you'll need special seeds for giant-sized pumpkins, such as 'Big Max' or 'Atlantic Giant', and a big garden space. You'll also need at least 4 months between spring planting (3 to 4 weeks after last frost) and fall harvest (after first frost). Add lots and lots of compost.

You'll need:

- compost
- pumpkin seeds for giant pumpkins
- compost tea
- straw mulch or newspapers

1 Using soil and compost, make four hills about 1 m (3 ft.) apart.

2 Plant three to four pumpkin seeds in each hill.

3 Once the shoots appear, choose the strongest-looking one and pull out the others, so that you have only one pumpkin growing in each hill.

4 When the plants bloom, remove all but three flowers (the flowers become the pumpkins). Those left on the vine will get more of everything — water, sun and nutrients.

5 Give the plants lots of water (warm water is best). Mulch with compost, and water with compost tea every few weeks.

6 As the pumpkins grow, put newspaper or straw mulch under them so they won't rot on moist soil. Turn the pumpkins so that they ripen on all sides. Let them grow and grow and grow.

Roasted pumpkin seeds

For a tasty treat, roast the pumpkin seeds that you scoop out of your jack-o'-lantern. First, wash the seeds and set them on a towel to dry. Spread the seeds on a cookie sheet, dribble a little vegetable oil over them and bake at 180°C (350°F) for about 10 minutes.

All manner of melons

Everybody loves one kind of melon or another. Here are some to try in your garden.

• *'Yellow Baby Hybrid' is a kid-sized, yellow watermelon with fewer seeds.*

• *'Alaska' and 'Earlisweet' are good varieties of cantaloupes for areas with short summers.*

• *'Earlidew' is a good honeydew melon for a short growing season.*

• *'Sugar Baby', 'Bush Jubilee', 'New Hampshire Midget' and 'Family Fun' are for smaller spaces and shorter summers.*

• *'Minnesota Midget' cantaloupe has a short vine and grows well in containers and small gardens.*

Watermelon Patch

Some old-time favorite watermelons grow vines that are 30 m (100 ft.) long. Now there are smaller varieties that you can grow in small gardens and in pots and barrels on a balcony. If your growing season is short, plant seedlings instead of seeds and pick a variety with a shorter growing season.

Melons need warm soil and temperatures, so wait until there's no danger of frost before starting your patch.

You'll need:
• compost
• 8 watermelon seeds or 2 seedlings (try 'Sugar Baby' in a small space)
• straw mulch
• compost tea

1 Dig two holes, about 15 cm (6 in.) deep and 1 m (3 ft.) apart. Fill the holes with compost.

2 On top of each hole, make a hill 15 to 20 cm (6 to 8 in.) high and 25 to 30 cm (10 to 12 in.) in diameter.

3 Sow four seeds per hill 2 to 3 weeks after the last frost date.

4 Thin to one plant per hill and mulch after the plants begin to grow.

5 Water the soil often.

6 Add compost tea after the fruits appear.

7 After the middle of summer, remove any new flowers because they won't have time to ripen.

8 Harvest the melon when the side that has been lying on the ground has turned from light yellow to gold or orange.

roma

beefsteak

cherry

Container tip

Plant cherry tomatoes or a dwarf variety, such as 'Pixie', in a pot.

Tomato Patch

Tomatoes come in all shapes and sizes, from tiny cherry tomatoes to huge beefsteaks that can weigh about a kilogram (2 to 3 lb.) each. They vary in color from yellow, orange or pink to bright red. Some, especially the large beefsteaks, need a long growing season. Cherry, dwarf and other varieties grow well in small gardens with short summers and will produce fruit a lot earlier.

There are two main types of tomatoes. Determinate types are bush-shaped tomato plants that produce one crop of tomatoes. They are a good choice for small spaces and containers. Indeterminate tomatoes grow long vines and keep producing fruit until frost. Indeterminate, or vine, tomatoes need support from tomato cages or stakes and string.

Planting a tomato patch

Plant tomatoes in full sun in a spot where you didn't grow tomatoes last year. By rotating your tomato patch, diseases will not get passed on in the soil.

You'll need:
- 3 tomato seedlings
- 3 tomato cages or stakes and string
- compost
- compost tea

1 About 2 to 3 weeks after the last frost date in your area, plant the seedlings about 60 cm (2 ft.) apart. The bottom leaves of the seedlings should be at soil level.

2 Place a tomato cage around each plant. If you're using stakes, sink the stake in the soil about 30 cm (1 ft.), and tie the stem of the seedling to the stake with string.

3 Mulch around the tomato plants with compost.

4 Water and weed regularly. Feed the plants compost tea every 3 weeks.

5 Tie the stems of vine tomatoes to stakes or wind them through the cage as they grow.

Cutworms can wipe out your tomato patch in one night by cutting through the stems of seedlings right at soil level. Protect your patch by making cutworm collars for your seedlings.

Remove the bottom from a paper cup. Place the paper cup ring over the tomato seedling and press it into the ground about 2.5 cm (1 in.). You can also use yogurt containers or frozen orange juice containers with bottoms removed.

Harvesting tips

• *When the tops of the green onions are about 15 cm (6 in.) tall, start pulling them. Leave a few bulbs in the ground — they'll go to seed and make plants for next year.*

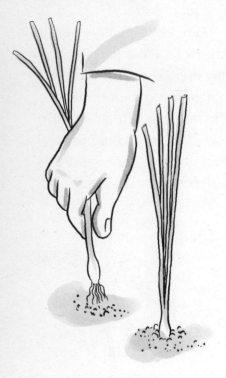

• *Cut the green shoots of garlic for salads, or harvest the whole bulb when the leaves are dry.*

• *Pick coriander leaves as you need them. Harvest the seeds at the end of the season.*

Salsa Garden

Add peppers, onions and garlic to your tomato patch, and you'll have all the ingredients to make your own spicy salsa. Peppers and tomatoes make great garden companions because they like the same conditions — full sun, a long, warm growing season, lots of rich soil and water.

Salsa garden plan

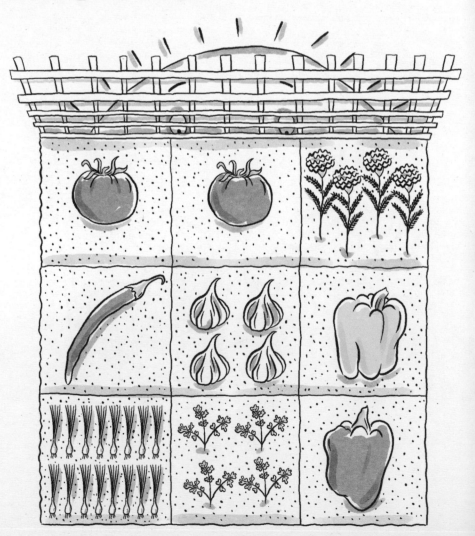

Planting your salsa garden

This garden is planted in squares, but use any style of planting you like. Try growing a salsa garden in a group of pots on your balcony.

You'll need:
- 16 green onion sets (bulbs)
- 4 garlic bulbs
- 2 tomato seedlings
- 1 chili pepper seedling
- 1 green pepper seedling
- 1 red pepper seedling
- 4 coriander seedlings
- 4 'Nugget' marigold seedlings
- compost tea
- tomato cages or stakes and string for vine tomatoes

1 Prepare a bed that is 1 m (3 ft.) square. Or place a group of large pots together in a sunny spot.

2 Using a measuring tape or just your eye, divide your large square into nine equal-sized smaller squares.

3 Two weeks before last spring frost, plant onion and garlic bulbs where they'll get some shade. When planted, the bulb tip should be just barely showing above the soil.

4 After the last frost date, plant the seedlings for tomatoes, peppers, coriander and marigolds.

5 Water well and add compost tea every 2 to 3 weeks.

6 Support vine tomatoes with cages or stakes and string.

Green thumb tip

Try this colorful mixture of lettuce varieties: 'Boston', 'Salad Bowl', 'Ruby Red', 'Oakleaf', 'Black-Seeded Simpson'. For mixed greens, try spinach, arugula and mustard.

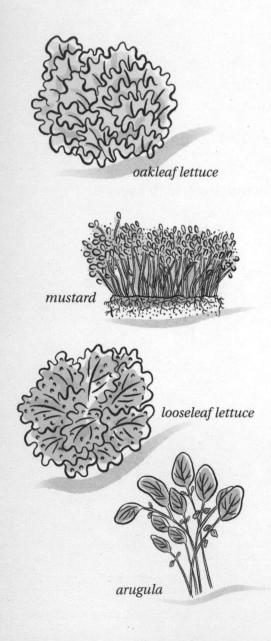

oakleaf lettuce

mustard

looseleaf lettuce

arugula

Mixed-Salad Basket

You can tuck some lettuce seeds or seedlings anywhere in your garden patch that gets a bit of shade in the afternoon. Or try this basketful of mixed lettuce and greens. You'll be eating a homegrown salad in no time.

Planting your basket

You'll need:
- wicker basket or other medium-sized container
- plastic shopping bag large enough to line bottom of the basket
- soil and compost
- variety of lettuce seeds or seedlings
- seeds for other mixed greens
- nasturtium seeds

1 Line the basket with the plastic bag and fill with soil and compost.

2 Sprinkle seeds for mixed greens and lettuce on top of the soil. Cover them very lightly with soil.

3 Because nasturtiums do not like to be moved, plant the seeds directly in your basket. The seeds should be covered well with soil.

4 Place the basket or container in a spot that gets some afternoon shade.

5 Spray the surface of the soil with warm water every day until the seeds sprout.

6 When the new seedlings are about 2.5 cm (about 1 in.) high, thin them to about 7 to 10 cm (3 to 4 in.) apart.

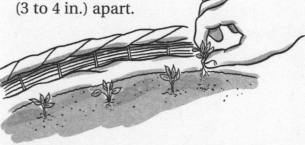

7 Water when the soil feels dry.

Scarecrow in Your Garden

What's a garden without a scarecrow, even if doesn't scare any crows away? Sit a homemade scarecrow on a chair in a sunny spot in your yard or on your balcony, and give it a vegetable garden all to itself.

There are many small varieties of vegetables that are just the right size for containers. These mini-vegetables usually grow faster and ripen sooner than larger varieties. When choosing plants or seeds, watch for varieties that say "baby-sized," "midget," "tiny," "little" or "mini."

Plant your mini-vegetables in a variety of recycled containers, such as an old hat, an old boot, large juice cans, milk cartons and jugs, old baskets, buckets and pots. Set them around, in and on your scarecrow.

Planting your scarecrow

You'll need:
- variety of old clothes
- plastic bags
- old leaves
- variety of recycled containers
- soil and compost mixture
- 'Tom Thumb' lettuce seeds
- 'Cherry Belle' radishes
- 'Mighty Midget' pea seeds
- 'Little Finger' carrot seeds
- 2 'Tiny Tim' tomato seedlings (or another variety of cherry tomatoes)
- compost tea

1 Use old pants, an old shirt, an old hat and gloves to make your own scarecrow. Stuff the pants, shirt and gloves with plastic bags or old leaves. Use a plastic bag to make a head and face. Sit your scarecrow on a chair in a sunny spot in your yard or balcony.

2 Make a few drainage holes in each container. Fill the containers with a mixture of soil and compost.

3 About 2 to 3 weeks before the last spring frost, sprinkle lettuce seeds on top of the soil in one of your containers and radish seeds in another.

4 At the same time, sow pea seeds 2.5 cm (1 in.) apart in another container. Sprinkle carrot seeds on top of the soil in a fourth container.

5 When the lettuce, radishes and carrots are 5 to 7 cm (2 to 3 in.) high, thin the seedlings so they are 5 cm (2 in.) apart.

6 About 2 to 3 weeks after last spring frost, plant tomato seedlings in a larger container. Use a stake to support the seedlings, if necessary.

7 Water often and fertilize with compost tea weekly.

 Container tip

You can also plant mini-vegetables in hanging baskets. Use a soilless mix to make the baskets lighter. Water the baskets whenever the surface feels dry, and add compost tea every 2 weeks.

Herbs for the Kitchen

Some herbs are grown to make perfume, medicine and insect repellent, but most gardeners grow herbs for the kitchen — to make teas and flavor food.

Your seed packets and seedling labels will tell you when to plant your herbs. Most herbs need warm temperatures and lots of sun.

Herbs grow well in small pots and tiny corners of the garden as long as they get the sunlight they need. Start by planting a few common herbs and keep adding two or three more each season.

Popular herbs

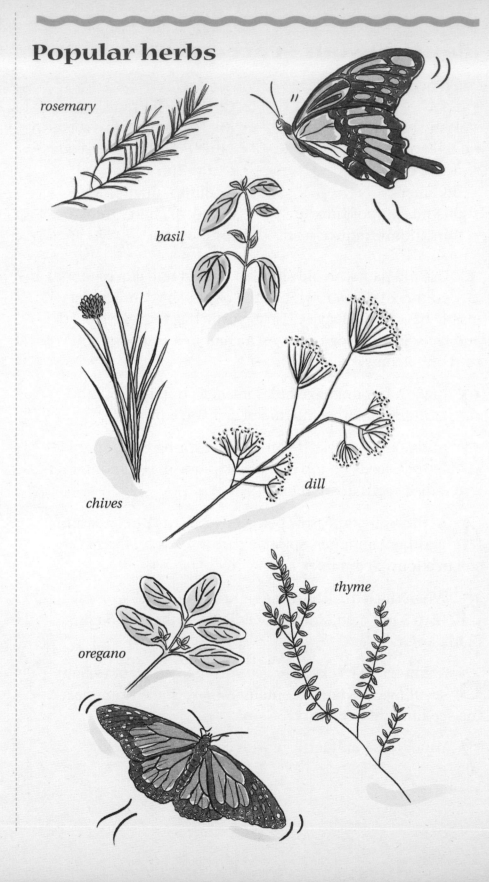

rosemary

basil

chives

dill

oregano

thyme

Broken-ladder herb garden

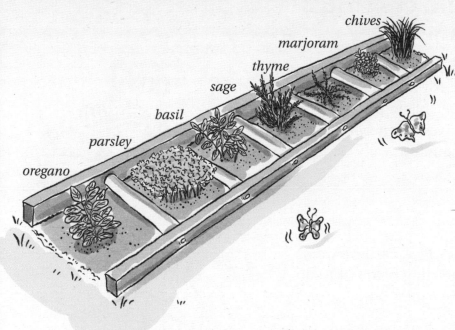

chives

marjoram

thyme

sage

basil

parsley

oregano

Pizza herb garden

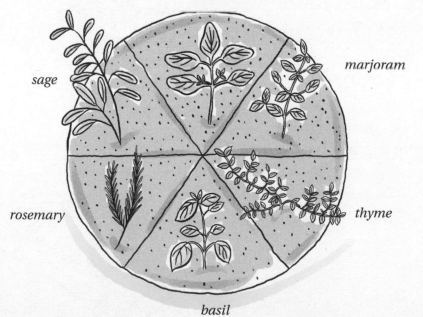

oregano

sage

marjoram

rosemary

thyme

basil

 Container tip

Parsley, marjoram, oregano, chives, thyme, rosemary and basil grow well in containers.

• *Basil was grown to keep witches away.*

• *Fennel seeds were placed in keyholes to prevent ghosts from getting in.*

• *Sprigs of dill were hung above the door to ward off evil spells.*

• *Pictures of thyme were embroidered on the scarves of knights to give them courage.*

Harvesting herbs

✿ When the plants look sturdy and are growing well, begin picking a few leaves whenever you need them.

✿ Pick herbs in the morning before the sun dries their oils.

✿ Regular picking makes the plants grow bushier.

✿ Always leave some leaves on the plant near the base of each stem so more leaves will grow.

✿ Wash the leaves and let them dry on a towel.

Drying herbs

✿ Harvest herbs for drying just as they form flower buds. Choose a day that's hot and sunny.

✿ Cut the plants off near the bottom of their main stem so that you get all the leaves.

✿ Wash the plants and dry them. Tie a string around the stems of two or three plants so they're attached in a bunch.

✿ Attach each bunch to a coat hanger, and hang it in a dark, dry place that has good air circulation. They will dry in about 2 weeks.

✿ Pick the leaves off the stems, keeping the leaves whole. Store them in labeled glass jars with lids in a dark, cool place.

Herbs have been used for thousands of years to heal wounds and make people feel better. These are some common old remedies: peppermint for indigestion, fennel for an upset stomach, lemon balm for sleep, chamomile and basil to calm nerves, and rosemary for headaches.

Make a pot of mint tea

Put about ten mint leaves in a teapot and add 500 mL (2 cups) of boiling water. Steep for about 10 minutes. You can also steep dried herbs in a tea ball. Use the same method for making other herbal teas. Combine a few herbs to create your own tea. Try some of these: chamomile flowers, lemon balm leaves, bergamot, sage and thyme.

Pole Bean Teepee

Bright red bean flowers make this a special hiding spot. Then you get to eat the beans.

You'll need:
- 6 bamboo poles at least 2 m (6 ft.) long
- twine or strong string
- scarlet runner bean seeds
- straw mulch

1 In a sunny spot in your garden, mark out a circle 1.2 m (4 ft.) in diameter.

2 Sink one end of each pole about 15 cm (about 6 in.) in the soil so they are evenly spaced around the circle. Leave a wider space between two poles for the door.

3 Have a helper hold the poles together at the top while you tie them together with twine or strong string.

4 Tie string to one of the poles that forms the door about 8 cm (3 in.) above the ground. Wrap string around and between each pole to make a web. Remember to leave the door open.

5 Make another string web about 20 cm (8 in.) above the first. Continue making string webs until you reach the top.

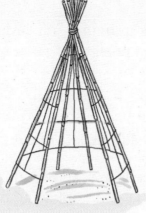

6 Plant bean seeds all around the teepee (but not at the door). Water well. Spread straw mulch inside.

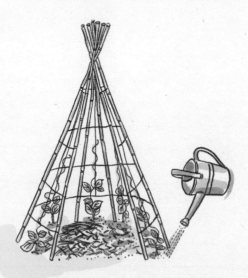

7 Carefully wind the bean vines through the string webbing as they grow. Water often.

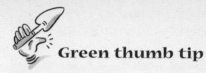

Green thumb tip

Plant sweet peas to share the same string and poles as the runner beans. Their flowers will attract bees to pollinate the beans' flowers. You can't have beans without pollinators.

Share your sunflower seeds

When the petals fall off the sunflowers, cut them off their stalks, leaving about 30 cm (1 ft.) of stalk on the flower. Leave them to dry until the stems stiffen. Then hang them outside to feed birds. You can also remove the seeds from the heads by rubbing them with your hand and putting the seeds into bird feeders. Save some for yourself.

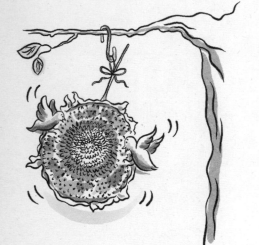

Sunflower Fort

Let the huge yellow flowers and big leaves protect you from the sun — and hide you away.

You'll need:
- compost
- measuring tape
- sunflower seeds, giant or mammoth variety
- 22 3 m (10 ft.) bamboo poles
- twine or strong string

1 Mark out a 2 m (6 ft.) square with small stakes and string. Prepare the soil by adding lots of compost.

2 Plant sunflower seeds in pairs about 5 cm (2 in.) apart every 30 cm (12 in.), following the string lines. Leave a 60 cm (2 ft.) space for a door. Water well.

3 When the seedlings are about 15 cm (6 in.) high, pull out the smaller plant in the pair, leaving one plant every 30 cm (12 in.).

4 When the sunflowers are about 1 m (3 ft.) tall, stake them with the bamboo poles and string. Keep tying them to the stakes as they grow.

5 In 2 months, you should have a fort with walls of sunflower stalks and leaves and a roof of sunflower heads.

What's a bramble?

Brambles are thorny shrubs that produce berries and live for about 20 years. Each year they grow new branches or canes. The canes grow berries in the second year and then die. Cut off (prune) the dead canes after you've picked the berries. When you buy canes from the nursery, they'll look like a stick with a few roots.

Other brambles and berries

There are different kinds of raspberries: summer-bearing red, ever-bearing red, black raspberries and yellow raspberries. In the south, give your raspberries some afternoon shade. Try growing heat-loving blackberries instead.

Raspberries and Other Brambles

Plant easy-to-grow raspberries in a sunny corner of your yard or against a fence. If you give them lots of compost, they'll grow into a thick, thorny bramble patch and be ready to harvest a year after planting. Be quick at harvesting your raspberries or the birds will beat you to them.

Planting a bramble patch

Plant raspberries early in the spring in a sunny spot soon after the last frost date. You can control your bramble patch by tying the bramble canes to a fence or trellis. It'll also save space, prevent disease and make it easier to pick berries and prune canes.

You'll need:
• compost   • 4 red raspberry canes   • mulch

1 Prepare a patch by adding lots of compost to the soil.

2 Dig holes deeper than the roots of the cane in a row about 1 m (3 ft.) apart along a fence and about 60 cm (2 ft.) from the fence.

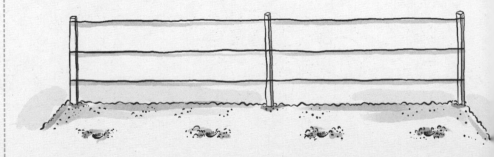

---

3 Plant the canes a bit deeper than they were growing in the nursery. (You can tell by the soil line left on the cane.)

4 Spread mulch around the canes to smother weeds and hold moisture in the soil.

5 Cut the canes back to about 15 cm (6 in.).

6 Water often, while the canes are growing and fruit is forming.

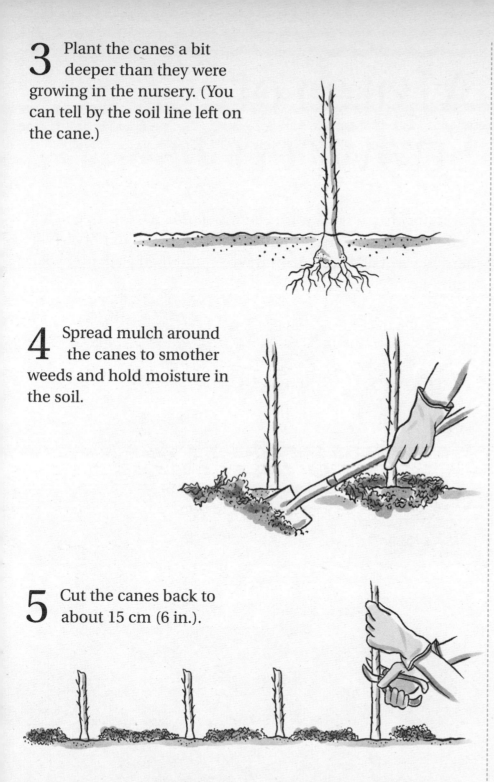

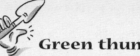

Green thumb tip

You can put netting over your brambles to prevent birds from harvesting berries before you do. Don't pick your berries when their leaves and fruit are wet from rain or dew.

Pruning raspberries

In the spring, cut out any canes that have died over the winter. Prune each cane to 120 cm (about 4 ft.) high. Thin your patch so that each new cane has room to grow and spread. In the fall, prune the canes that have already produced berries.

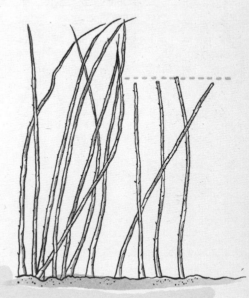

A pot of strawberries

Strawberries are such a garden favorite that there are special pots to grow them in. Set a strawberry pot in a sunny spot on your balcony.

A Patch of Strawberries

Plant strawberries in a warm, sunny spot in a weed-free patch of well-composted, well-drained soil. You can start harvesting berries a year after you plant them — and then year after year after year.

Planting your patch

You'll need:
- compost or manure
- 10 ever-bearing strawberry plants
- straw mulch

1 Add lots of compost to the soil.

2 Plant five plants in each row 30 cm (12 in.) apart. Plant a second row 60 cm (2 ft.) away. Be sure not to bury the crown (center) of the plants. Mulch between rows and water well.

3 For the first 3 months after planting, remove the flowers to give the plants a chance to grow sturdy. For the first 2 years, remove all the runners (the new offshoots).

4 After the ground freezes in the fall, cover the plants with straw to protect them. Remove the mulch from the plants in early spring.

5 After 3 years, let the runners grow to form new rows and remove the older plants in the fall.

WARNING!

Don't eat rhubarb leaves — they're poisonous.

A rhubarb harvest

Start harvesting your rhubarb in early spring a year after planting the crown. The stalks should be about 30 cm (12 in.) long, and the leaves should be completely open. Grab each stalk at the crown, twist and pull.

When harvesting your rhubarb, take along a sugar bowl. There's nothing better than nibbling a rhubarb stalk dipped in sugar.

Rhubarb Patch

Plant rhubarb once, and it will reappear every year in your garden. Rhubarb stalks are one of the earliest spring treats you can harvest.

Rhubarb grows best in a sunny spot. It likes cooler temperatures and cold winters. Plant a piece of rhubarb root, or a crown, in early spring. The crown should have one or more buds (called eyes).

You'll need:
• compost   • a rhubarb crown   • mulch

1 Dig a deep, wide hole, about 60 cm (2 ft.) wide and deep.

2 Fill the hole to within 5 cm (2 in.) of the top with a mixture of soil and compost.

3 Place the rhubarb root in the soil so that the crown (center) is 5 cm (2 in.) below the surface. Fill the rest of the hole with soil. Pat down the soil. Water well.

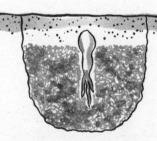

4 Add mulch once the plants have grown.

5 Later in the summer flower stalks will grow. Remove them to encourage more leaf growth.

6 In the second year, harvest when leaf stalks are at least 2.5 cm (1 in.) thick.

Planting Potatoes

This is one vegetable that isn't grown from seeds or from seedlings. If you want to grow your own potatoes, you'll have to plant potato "eyes." These eyes are potato buds, and they grow into potato stems.

You can buy seed potatoes at a gardening center, or plant potatoes from your kitchen. (Use chemical-free potatoes.)

You'll need:
- potatoes • knife

1 Cut each potato into four pieces, making sure each piece has at least two eyes. Let the pieces sit for a few days before planting.

2 Plant the potato pieces 10 cm (4 in.) deep — with the eyes pointing up — about 30 cm (12 in.) apart.

3 As the plant grows, mound soil up around it to prevent the growing potatoes from being exposed to sunlight. They turn green with too much light, and the green part can make you sick.

4 After the plant stems and leaves die in the fall, it's time to dig up your potatoes.

A Victory Garden

During World War Two, people helped the war effort by planting Victory Gardens in their backyards and in vacant lots in cities and towns all across North America. These Victory Gardens provided about half the crops needed to feed people on the homefront.

When you've got some vegetable-growing experience under your belt, put it all together and plant a Victory Garden. You'll harvest enough vegetables to help feed four people all summer long.

1 Divide each of the 2 garden plots into 16 equal squares.

2 Plant lettuce, peas, green onions, carrots, parsley and radishes before the last frost date.

3 Plant beans, zucchini and other squash, potatoes, tomatoes, cucumbers, peppers, basil, marigolds and nasturtiums after the last frost date. If your growing season is short, plant seedlings.

4 Install a trellis at the north end of the two plots for the tomatoes, cucumbers, peas and beans.

5 Plant the corn in three rows next to the plots.

6 For the squash, make four hills, add lots of compost and plant the seeds.

7 Water, weed and add compost tea.

You'll need:
- 2 small garden plots, each 1.2 m (4 ft.) square
- an area for corn, 1 m (3 ft.) square
- 4 hills for squash at least 1 m (3 ft.) apart
- 16 leaf lettuce seeds
- 24 snap pea seeds
- 32 green onion bulbs
- 32 carrot seeds
- 4 parsley seedlings
- 16 radish seeds
- 18 pole bean seeds
- 18 yellow bush beans
- 1 zucchini seed
- 1 acorn squash seed
- 1 butternut squash seed
- 1 pumpkin seed
- 2 potato pieces with eyes
- 2 vine tomato seedlings
- 8 cherry tomato seedlings
- 4 cucumber seeds
- 3 sweet red pepper seedlings
- 8 basil seedlings
- 4 marigold seeds
- 4 nasturtium seeds
- 9 corn seeds

Plan for a Victory Garden

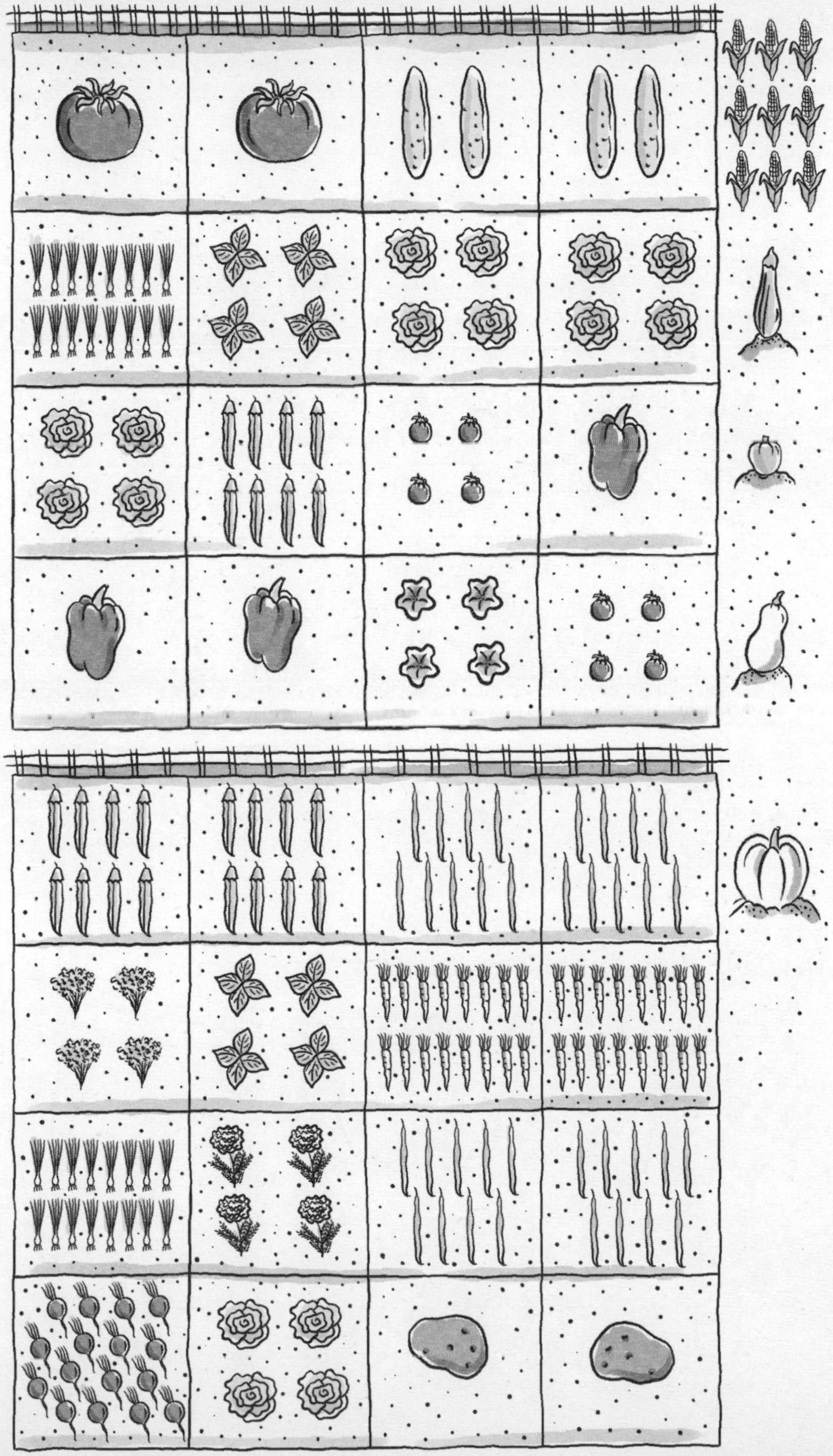

vine tomatoes

green onions
basil

leaf lettuce
snap peas

sweet red peppers

cucumbers
corn

leaf lettuce
zucchini

cherry tomatoes
sweet red peppers
acorn squash

nasturtium
cherry tomatoes
butternut squash

snap peas

parsley
basil

green onions
marigold

radishes
leaf lettuce

pole beans
pumpkin

carrots

yellow bush beans

potatoes

Flower Gardens

Most flowers are grown just for their beautiful blooms and sweet smells. When you're looking for a good place to plant flowers, find a spot where you'll see and smell them the most. Tuck some marigolds in a vegetable patch, plant a few sweet peas in a pot on your porch, grow morning glories up a fence, or create your own bed of roses in the backyard.

Favorite Flowers

If you look at flower gardens in your neighborhood, you'll see a lot of the same plants. They are usually flowers that are easy to grow in your area and to buy as seeds or seedlings at a garden center. Start with a small garden and grow a few of your neighborhood's favorite flowers.

Annual favorites

Annual plants go from being seeds in the spring to producing seeds in the fall. After completing their one-year life cycle, they die.

Annual flowers are very easy to grow from both seeds and seedlings (seedlings are also called bedding plants). They bloom in almost any color, and many bloom all summer long. If you plant annual seeds in the spring, you'll have flowers in midsummer. If you plant seedlings, you'll get flowers faster. Many plants that are called tender perennials, such as fuchsia and snapdragon, are treated like annuals because they can't survive the cold winters.

Here are five annual favorites that are easy to grow from seed in most areas.

✿ Cornflower

The small, round blue flowers of this plant (also called bachelor's button and bluebottle) bloom from early summer until frost. Other varieties have purple, white or pink flowers. New cornflowers will grow next year if you let some flowers go to seed. The seeds will germinate when the soil warms up in the spring, and the sun-loving plants will grow right through a hot, dry summer.

✿ Nasturtium

Nasturtium got its Latin name — "nose twister" — because of its strong smell. Nasturtiums bloom about 50 days after the seeds are planted, in orange, yellow and red. There are trailing varieties that grow long stems (60 cm or about 2 ft.) for hanging baskets and shorter varieties (30 cm or about 1 ft.) for tucking in almost anywhere. They grow well in sunny, dry places with poor soil. You can eat the flowers, so try adding them to your salad bowl.

✿ Morning glory

Morning glories are climbing flower vines that grow from 2.5 to 4 m (about 8 to 12 feet). The flowers are mostly blue, white or pink and open at sunrise. The vines need a support to climb up. They'll wind themselves around strings and bamboo poles on your balcony or through the fence in your backyard.

Green thumb tip

Pinch off the dead flower heads of annuals, such as sweet pea, cosmos, snapdragon, salvia and zinnia, and they'll grow more flowers. This is called deadheading.

❀ Cosmos

This is another annual that likes full sun and doesn't mind dry, poor soil. It blooms from midsummer until frost. The leaves are feathery, and the flowers are pink, white or red. Leave a few flowers to produce seeds. They'll fall onto the soil and grow new cosmos next year.

❀ Snapdragon

Snapdragons are called snapdragons because their flowers are hinged, and when you squeeze the hinge, a big dragon-mouth opens and a long tongue snaps out. They come in lots of colors (red, orange, yellow, pink, white and crimson), and there are varieties that grow short (15 cm or about 6 in.) and tall (1 m or about 3 ft.).

Favorite annuals from seedlings

Here are some favorite annuals that most gardeners grow from seedlings rather than seeds: petunia, impatiens, pansy, marigold, lobelia, geranium.

Perennial favorites

The best thing about perennials is that you have to plant them only once. The stem, leaves and flowers die each winter, but the root survives in the ground. It sends up new stems, leaves and flowers in the spring. While most annuals bloom all summer long, many perennials bloom for just a few weeks.

Perennials take a long time to grow from seed, so most gardeners plant perennial seedlings in their gardens. Perennials will bloom in your garden year after year if you plant them in the right spot. Add lots of compost to the soil before you plant them. Add mulch (don't let it touch the stems) to hold water in the soil and control weeds.

✿ Purple coneflower

This is a beautiful native North American plant. Its pinky-purple flowers bloom a little earlier than black-eyed Susans do. It stands 60 to 100 cm (about 2 to 3 ft.) tall.

✿ Solomon's seal

This native perennial prefers a very shady, moist spot. It grows about 60 to 100 cm (2 to 3 ft.) tall. Its tiny white flowers hang like little slippers from the underside of the stem.

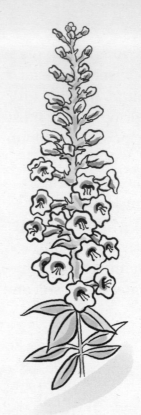

🌼 Yarrow

Yarrow arrived in North America from Europe and now grows wild in many areas. It's a tall plant (about 60 to 100 cm or 2 to 3 ft.), with large, flat-topped yellow flowers that bloom from late spring until midsummer. The leaf is feathery and gray-green in color. There are many varieties of yarrow that have white, pink or red flowers.

🌼 Foxglove

Foxglove is really a biennial, which is a plant that takes two years to produce seeds. A native of Europe, it now grows as a wildflower in North America. It's a very tall plant (120 cm or 4 ft.) with pinky-purple, bell-like flowers that hang on the stalk in late spring until early summer. Foxgloves need some shade, moist, well-drained soil and lots of compost.

🌼 Black-eyed Susan

This all-time favorite is native to North America. Its composite flower is made up of dark brown disc flowers in the center that are surrounded by yellow ray flowers. It blooms from midsummer until fall on stems that grow 60 to 90 cm (about 2 to 3 ft.) tall.

❀ Dividing old perennials

When your perennials aren't growing as well as they used to, it's time to divide them.

1 In fall (or spring in cooler areas), dig up the whole plant — root and all.

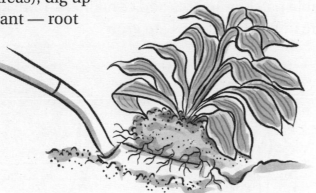

2 Pull off young shoots from the old clump of roots. If it's too tough to separate the new shoots by hand, carefully cut them apart with a knife or shovel. Be sure each section has a root.

3 Plant the new sections as soon as possible and water well.

Shady perennials

Don't despair if your garden spot doesn't get full sun. Here's a list of flowering perennials that will bloom in the shade.

> *foxglove*
> *columbine*
> *obedient plant*
> *daylilies*
> *bleeding heart*
> *crane's bill*
> *violet*

> *Solomon's seal*
> *foamflower*
> *trillium*
> *hostas*
> *lily of the valley*

100 What's a bulb?

A bulb is a swollen underground stem. Inside it is a bud surrounded by layers of scales that store food. Most bulbs are planted in the fall. They'll survive the winter underground and start to grow stems and leaves in spring.

 **Green thumb tip**

Squirrels and mice love eating bulbs just after you've planted them. But they don't like daffodils, so plant lots of them if these creatures dig in your garden. You can also try planting your other bulbs deeper to keep creatures from digging them up.

Favorite bulbs

Bulbs are the first flowers to bloom in the spring and a cheerful reminder that winter is over. Bulbs can be planted almost anywhere — in a flower bed, a herb garden, a vegetable patch or in pots and containers. Here are some favorite bulbs that are easy to grow.

tulip

hyacinth

daffodil

crocus

❀ Planting and tending bulbs

Bulbs like a sunny spot, well-drained soil and lots of compost. Plant bulbs close together in groups or clusters.

1 Dig a hole that's three times the depth of the bulb.

2 Add a handful of compost or bonemeal to the hole.

3 Place the bulb in the hole with its pointed side up and root side down.

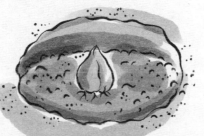

4 Fill in the hole with soil and water well.

5 In spring, put compost around the plant after its stem and leaves appear.

6 After the plants have finished blooming, let the leaves turn brown and fall over before removing them. The leaves feed the bulb so it will grow next year.

Allium (flowering onion)

Allium is a kind of onion with flowers that bloom in early summer. Giant Onion grows to 120 cm (4 ft.) tall in full sun. The variety called 'Purple Sensation' has huge purple flower balls and grows about 90 cm (3 ft.) tall. Moly is a short onion with tiny yellow flowers. Alliums make great dried flowers.

 **Container tip**

Plant daffodils, grape hyacinth, and tulips in outdoor containers. In areas with cold winters, use deep containers and cover bulbs with an extra layer of soil.

Flower checklist:

Name of plant: _____

_____

_____

Perennial ____ /Annual ____

Hardiness zone: _____

Color: _____

When it blooms: _____

Full sun ____ /

Part shade ____ /

Full shade ____ /

Height: _____

Width: _____

Special features: _____

_____

_____

_____

_____

_____

_____

_____

_____

Planning and Designing

Start planning your flower garden by making flower checklists. Look at what's growing in your neighbors' gardens or a flower-filled park. Find your favorites in plant and seed catalogs and make a flower checklist for each one. Then start drawing your garden plan.

Drawing a garden plan

Whether you're growing flowers for the first time or the sixteenth, it's a good idea to make a scale drawing of your garden. It's much easier to move pictures of plants around a paper garden than it is to move real plants around a real garden.

1 Draw the size and shape of your garden to scale on paper.

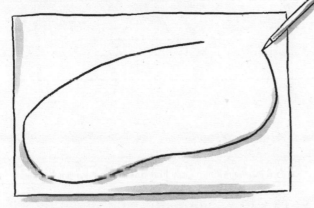

2 On another piece of paper, draw circles to scale for each of the plants on your checklist. Draw as many plants of each kind or variety as you want.

3 Cut out your plant circles and color them. You may also cut out pictures of your plants from plant catalogs, making each cutout to scale.

4 Place your cutouts on your garden plan, and move them around until you've got a design you like.

Your own creation

Create a flower garden that's a living work of art by experimenting with the color, size, shape and even the scent of your plants. You might want to try some of the ideas other gardeners have used to make their garden creations beautiful and interesting.

❁ Put at least three plants of the same kind together in a group or clump, rather than spreading them out in a row.

❁ Vary the height of plants, with the taller ones at the back of a border and in the center of a bed.

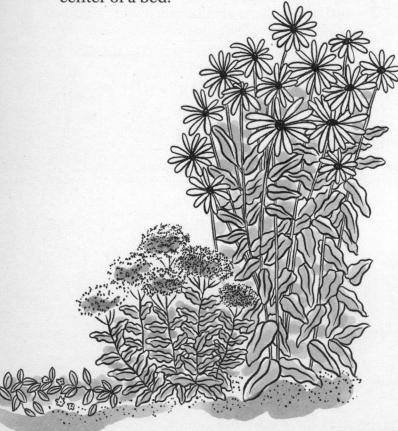

❁ Use a variety of flower shapes: something round, such as thistle; something flat, such as yarrow; something tall and spiky, such as blazing star; and something with lots of petals, such as black-eyed Susan.

Designing with color

❁ Create a color pattern by repeating the same color in a few different spots.

❁ Plant hot colors — red, orange and yellow — together to create a cheerful garden. Plant cool colors — white, blue, purple and green — together to create a peaceful garden.

❁ Use white flowers to lighten shady spots.

❁ Plant flowers with contrasting, or complementary colors, such as purple and yellow or red and green, side by side. Purple and yellow are a good complementary color combination for attracting butterflies.

❁ Plant flowers that are different shades of the same color together.

Beds, Borders and Baskets

Flower gardens come in all shapes and sizes, and half the fun of growing flowers is deciding how to plant them. Find a spot for your garden, and then give it whatever shape strikes your fancy. Be sure to choose a variety of plants that flower at different times so your garden blooms all summer long.

✿ Blooming borders

A border is a garden planted against a wall or fence. Start with a border that's 1 m (about 3 ft.) long. Grow some climbing flowers up a fence or on bamboo poles at the back of your border.

✿ Blooming beds

A bed is an island of garden that you can walk around. A good size to start with is 60 cm by 100 cm (about 2 ft. by 3 ft.).

✿ Blooming baskets

Containers look best when they're overflowing with flowers, but they dry out quickly so fill them with plants that can handle dry conditions. Choose a plastic, wicker or wire container, and instead of soil, fill it with a soilless mix.

Make a hanging basket for spring by planting grape hyacinth, ivy, pansy and primula.

Ox-eye daisy

Ox-eye daisies are easy to grow and make some of the best bouquets. They are native to Europe and Asia and now grow wild in North America. The plant's name started as "day's eye" because daisies open when the sun rises and close when it sets.

The petals you pull off an ox-eye daisy aren't really petals. They are tiny flowers called ray flowers. The yellow center of the daisy is made up of disc flowers. A daisy is a composite flower, which means it's really hundreds of tiny flowers.

Homegrown Bouquets

Grow lots of beautiful blooms for your own bouquets. With many annual flowers, the more you pick, the more you get. Some flowers are more pickable than others. They are called "cut flowers" in plant books and seed catalogs.

lily

purple coneflower

Queen Anne's lace

cornflower

zinnia

❀ Good picks

Flowers with long stems and large blooms that last a long time are good for cutting and then displaying in vases. Try planting some of these: lilac, rose, aster, zinnia, foxglove, chrysanthemum, geranium, daisy, cosmos, lily, coreopsis, snapdragon, cornflower, black-eyed Susan, purple coneflower, iris, baby's breath, yarrow, Queen Anne's lace, tulip, allium, spider flower.

❀ Bouquet tips

- Cut flower stems with scissors to avoid damaging the plant.
- Choose blooms that are not fully open — they'll last longer.
- Cut flowers first thing in the morning or late in the afternoon when they're not wilting in the hot sun.
- Cut as long a stem as you can, and cut it on an angle.
- If flowers wilt, recut their stems and add a tablet of Aspirin to fresh warm water.
- Put daffodils and daisies in vases by themselves. Their stems gives off poisons that kill other flowers.
- Drop a penny in a vase of tulips to keep the flowers from opening too quickly.

Green thumb tip

Poppies, petunias, marigolds and woodland wildflowers wilt quickly and don't make good cut flowers.

Tiny flowers for tiny vases

You can use clean perfume bottles, salt and pepper shakers, frozen-juice containers, pill bottles and juice glasses for bouquets of small flowers, such as snowdrop, pansy, forget-me-not, violet, clover, buttercup, sweet pea and sweet William.

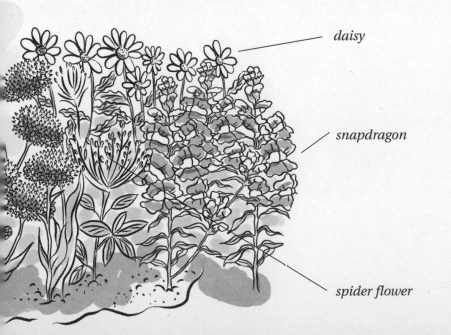

daisy

snapdragon

spider flower

Violets

Sweet violets are famous for their fragrance. They were brought to North America from Europe. Two other European violets are Johnny-jump-up and the pansy. There are 70 different kinds of native North American violets. They grow well in moist, shady spots, and many spread very easily.

Sweet-Smelling Garden

Flowers have sweet smells to attract bees and other pollinators. Bees can usually smell a flower long before it comes into view. The smell comes from oils in the flowers or leaves. Some flowers are more powerfully scented than others. Sometimes you have to put your nose right up to a flower or crush a leaf to smell its scent. The best time for smelling flowers in the air is a damp day that isn't too windy or too hot.

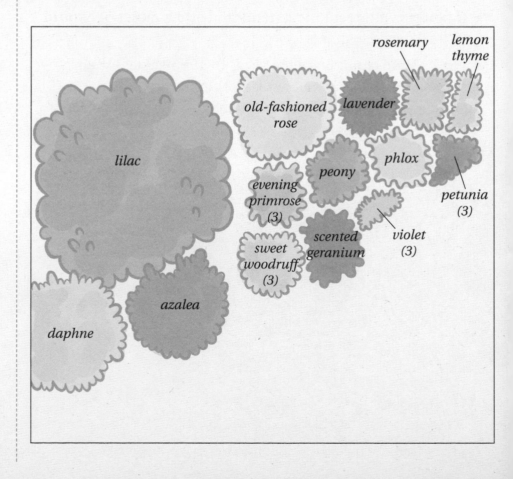

❧ Stinkers

Some plants and flowers smell horrible because the insects that pollinate them like horrible smells. Many flies, for example, are attracted to the smell of rotting meat. The fruit on the female ginkgo smells so bad that most creatures just leave it alone. Some poisonous plants, such as poison sumach and Jimsonweed, have an odor that warns off hungry creatures.

Here are some stinkers to try (or not) in your garden: carrion flower, skunk cabbage, stinkweed, stinking cranesbill, feverfew, crown imperial fritillary, pickerel weed, bugbane.

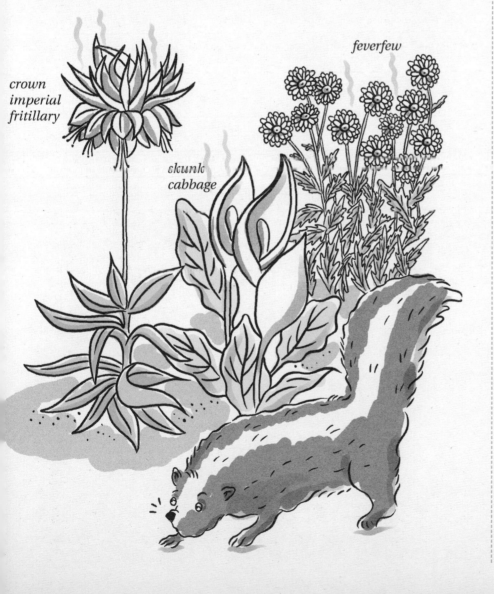

crown imperial fritillary

skunk cabbage

feverfew

Try some of these sweet-smelling plants:

• **Herbs:** *lavender, lemon thyme, sage, lemon balm, peppermint, rosemary*

• **Perennials:** *phlox, peony, bee balm, violet, artemisia, sweet woodruff, evening primrose, yucca*

• **Annuals:** *scented geranium, nicotiana, sweet alyssum, sweet pea, petunia, verbena, four o'clock, moonflower, nasturtium*

• **Bulbs:** *hyacinth, regal and Madonna lilies, daffodil*

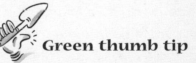 **Green thumb tip**

Grow old-fashioned (original) species of plants. They have a stronger smell than cultivars or hybrids.

This night-blooming plant is also known as Adam's needle, silk grass and bear's grass because of the plant's spiky leaves with their fine threads. Native North Americans used thread made from yucca leaves to weave cloth and make rope and baskets. The plant can be fertilized only by the female yucca moth. She makes her egg case from the pollen of one flower and lays the egg case in another flower, fertilizing it in the process. This plant looks very tropical but it survives well in cooler areas too. The yucca is a good container plant because it can handle dry conditions.

Night-Blooming Garden

Flowers that bloom at night catch the moon's glow and fill the air with wonderful scents. They also attract lots of nighttime creatures looking for sweet nectar.

Creatures of the night

Switch on garden or porch lights and watch for these flying creatures.

❀ Moths

Moths are important pollinators. They are attracted to white flowers with deep lobes, such as angel's trumpet, hosta and moonflower vine. They also like the evening scent of native honeysuckle, nicotiana, evening primrose, night-scented stock and red valerian. Just like butterfly caterpillars, moth larvae need special host plants, such as willow, poplar, privet, lilac, apple, legumes and bird's foot trefoil.

❀ Fireflies

The firefly, also called a lightning bug, is a beetle that brings its own light to a nighttime garden. The light it creates is a mating signal. Fireflies hide out in long grass and are a rare sight today because of bug-killing pesticides and lawn mowers. If you let your grass grow long — and don't use pesticides — fireflies may light up your garden.

A crescent moon–shaped garden

Nicotiana (tobacco plant)

The night-flowering nicotiana has clusters of beautiful flowers that bloom well in a shady spot for most of the summer. Plant the old-fashioned white variety. It grows about 1 m (about 3 ft.) tall and is very fragrant at night.

Night bloomers

Moonflower, evening primrose, delphinium, dame's rocket, hibiscus, campion, night-scented stock, four-o'clock, night phlox, madonna lily, night-scented catchfly, yucca, nicotiana

Everlasting Garden

Flowers bloom only for a short time, but you can make them last longer by picking and drying them. Arrange the dried flowers in a vase or pot, and they will bloom all year long. Here are some plants to try in your everlasting garden.

statice   *strawflower*   *yarrow*   *baby's breath*

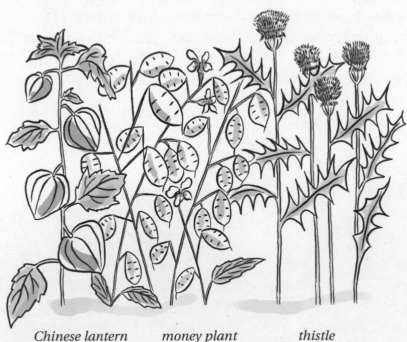

Chinese lantern   *money plant*   *thistle*

Drying flowers

Choose a dry day, and begin cutting almost-open blooms after the morning dew is gone but before the sun wilts them.

1 Cut the flower stems, leaving them at least 30 cm (12 in.) long.

2 Tie the stems in small bunches with an elastic band.

3 Hang them in a dark, dry, well-ventilated place for 2 to 4 weeks. Darkness prevents the flowers from fading. The bunches of flowers shouldn't touch each other.

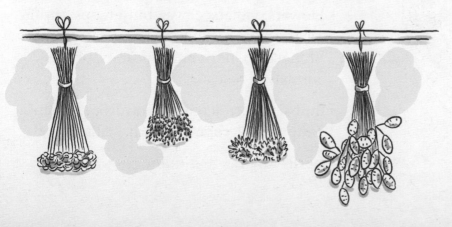

Strawflower

This annual's yellow, red, orange or purple flowers bloom from mid to late summer. The central petals are surrounded by papery petals that are actually bracts or scale-like leaves. Strawflowers have a weak stem that you can replace with a piece of thin wire.

Everlasting plants

Try some of these everlastings: statice, strawflower, cornflower, yarrow, lavender, teasel, tansy, baby's breath, hydrangea, pussy toes, rose, black-eyed Susan, milkweed, Chinese lantern, allium, money plant, poppy, thistle, grasses.

Miniature Garden

If you want paths and ponds and lots of plants but you don't have a big space, create this miniature garden in a container. It's got everything a large garden has, but in a scaled-down size. Add small stones or pebbles to represent boulders, sand to make a path and a mirror to make a pond. Create a scene by adding a small house or fort.

You'll need:

- soil
- shallow container
- 1 thyme plant
- 6 grape hyacinth bulbs
- 1 marjoram plant
- 3 hens and chickens plants
- 3 rosemary plants
- mirror
- sand
- river pebbles or small rocks

1 Add soil to the container until it is two-thirds full.

2 Plant the plants, leaving space for a path and rocks.

3 Press the mirror into the soil and cover the edges with soil.

4 Sprinkle sand over the soil to make a path.

5 Place the pebbles or small rocks near the mirror.

6 Water the plants often.

❀ Tiny plants

- **Flowers:** violets, clover, buttercups, thrift, saxifrage or rockfoil, sedum (also called stonecrop), hens and chickens, phlox, miniature roses

- **Bulbs:** winter aconite, snowdrops, crocus, tulip tarda, grape hyacinth, scilla

- **Herbs:** thyme, marjoram, rosemary

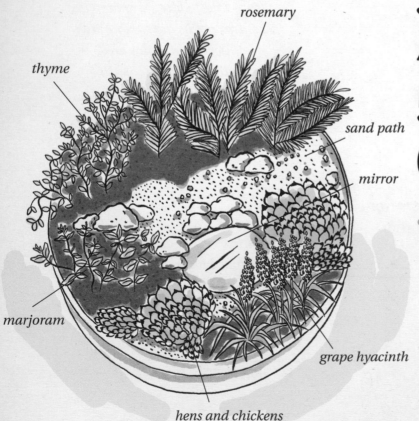

thyme

rosemary

sand path

mirror

marjoram

grape hyacinth

hens and chickens

Growing Grasses

Plant grasses that you won't have to mow every week. Many grasses that are native to North America work well in dry garden sites and are good plants to grow for gardeners who want to conserve water. Other grasses thrive in wet locations.

The seed heads of grasses will look great in your garden over the winter. Best of all, grasses require very little tending. Just cut your grass patch once a year in early spring to about 5 cm (2 in.).

❀ Seed heads will attract birds to your garden. Try big bluestem, sideoats grama, little bluestem, prairie dropseed or switchgrass.

switchgrass

❀ Help preserve native grasses by planting them in your garden. Try big bluestem, little bluestem, Indian grass, switchgrass and California fescue.

❀ Grasses add interesting colors and shapes to a flower garden. Try blue fescue, Japanese blood grass, blue oat grass, zebra grass or purple fountain grass.

❀ Plant tall grasses at the back of a border or in the center of a bed. Try these tall ones: big bluestem, switchgrass or Indian grass.

❀ Plant pampas, giant miscanthus and giant reed in containers so they won't take over your garden.

fountain grass

This plant is rose-shaped and has lots of baby rosettes growing around it — making it look like a hen surrounded by her baby chicks. It thrives in a rock garden, where it quickly sends its offspring, or off-shoots, spreading into every nook and cranny. Because it is a succulent plant with thick leaves that hold water, it's a favorite choice for dry, hot rock gardens.

This plant is also called roof houseleek because it was planted on thatch roofs of houses in Europe. People believed that the plant protected their houses from lightning. Some believed that a thatch roof full of hens and chickens meant they would never be poor.

Rock Garden

A hilly slope is a good place for a rock garden, but you can make one wherever there's lots of sun and good drainage. Find some large rocks, and set them close together. For a natural look, bury a third of each rock in the soil. If you don't have room for large rocks, use rounded stones as a mulch around your plants. Plants that grow well in rock gardens are small and compact. Try planting dwarf iris or daffodil, grape hyacinth, anemone, alyssum, ajuga, sedum, rock cress, hens and chickens, candytuft, saxifrage, pinks, bellflower, mother of thyme, pussy toes and basket of gold.

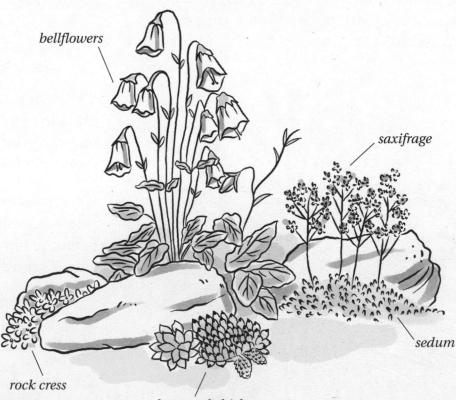

bellflowers

saxifrage

sedum

rock cress

hens and chickens

Shoe Full of Flowers

Do you have an old pair of running shoes that are too special to throw out? Turn them into a pair of planters.

You'll need:
- hammer and nail
- an old running shoe (or two)
- potting soil
- 2 lobelia seedlings
- 2 marguerite seedlings
- 2 pansy seedlings
- fish emulsion, compost or manure tea

1 With the hammer and nail, make several drainage holes in the bottom of an old shoe.

2 Fill the bottom and toe of the shoe with potting soil.

3 Position the plants in the opening of the shoe, with the taller marguerites in the middle, the pansies at the side and the trailing lobelia at the edge.

4 Fill in around the plants with more soil, pressing the plants firmly in place.

5 Water often and fertilize with fish emulsion, compost or manure tea every few weeks.

Monkey flower

This native plant has been hybridized to produce many different varieties. It has trumpet-shaped flowers that are yellow with red or brown dots, which make it look like a monkey's face. It grows to about 30 cm (1 ft.) in fertile soil with full sun.

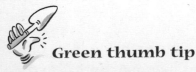

Green thumb tip

Here is a good combination of flowers for baskets that hang in the shade: fuchsia, begonia, impatiens, lobelia.

Hanging Garden

If you haven't got any space on the ground to garden, you can hang your garden up — on a fence, on a balcony, on a porch or in a tree. If you live in an area with cold winters, plant mostly annuals in your hanging baskets. If you plant perennials, take your basket indoors for the winter.

A hanging garden needs to be light, so choose plastic, wicker or metal wire baskets and try to use a soilless mix instead of garden soil.

monkey flower

marigold

nasturtium

Make a hanging garden

You can make your own container by recycling an old colander.

You'll need:
- 4 small S hooks
- 4 45 cm (18 in.) lengths of small-link chain
- an old colander
- 1 bag of sphagnum moss
- 1 small bag of soilless mix
- 2 pails
- 3 monkey flower seedlings
- 3 marigold seedlings
- 2 trailing nasturtium seedlings
- 1 large S hook
- fish emulsion or compost tea

1 Using the small S hooks, attach two chains to the handles of the colander. Attach the other two chains by hooking the S hooks into two holes located high in the colander on the sides that are opposite the handles.

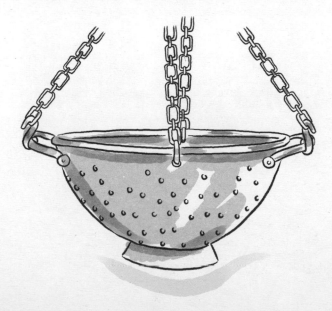

2 Place both the moss and soilless mix in separate pails. Add enough water to moisten them. Let them sit for a few hours.

3 Squeeze out any excess water from the moss. Line the colander with the moss to a thickness of about 5 cm (2 in.) on the bottom and 2.5 cm (1 in.) on the sides.

4 Add soilless mix so that the moss-lined colander is two-thirds full.

5 Plant the monkey flower in the center and the marigolds and trailing nasturtium around the outside. You want the colander to look full so add more plants and soilless mix if necessary.

6 Attach all the chains together on the large S hook, making sure that the colander hangs evenly. Hang it up.

7 Water the container often, daily when it's hot. Fertilize with fish emulsion or compost tea every few weeks.

Green thumb tips

• *Some people say that burying banana skins around rose bushes makes the roses bloom better. This could be true because banana skins contain magnesium, sulfur, calcium and phosphates, which improve the soil and feed the roses.*

• *In hot weather, water the roses well in the mornings, and give them compost tea a few times a year.*

Garden of Old Roses

Of all the plants in the world, the rose is probably the most well known and best loved. Because of its beauty and sweet fragrance, it's been a symbol of romantic love for thousands of years.

Choose "old roses" for your garden — they are easier to grow than the new hybrid varieties.

❀ Old roses

"Old" roses are old compared to the new hybrid or tea roses, which were introduced in 1867. Old roses are often called "heritage" or "historical" roses. They are much hardier than hybrid roses. They resist diseases better, need less care and have a stronger fragrance.

climbing rose

shrub rose

bush rose

native rose

Making a rose bed

Roses need a sunny garden site with good air circulation and no tree roots nearby. In areas with cold winters, plant roses in early spring. In warm areas, plant them in the fall.

You'll need:
- 1 'Tuscany Superb' bush rose
- 1 'Blanc Double de Coubert' bush rose
- 1 'Old Pink Moss' bush rose
- compost
- mulch
- compost tea

1 Dig three holes 60 cm (2 ft.) deep and 60 cm (2 ft.) wide, about 1 m (3 ft.) apart.

2 Remove each rose from its pot without disturbing its roots, and set it in a hole.

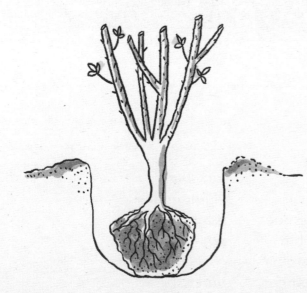

3 Fill in the holes and around the plants with compost, and build a moat around each plant to hold water. Water well. Add mulch.

4 In areas with cold winters, make a soil mound around the stem of the roses in the fall to protect them from freezing and thawing. Remove the mounds in the spring.

Special Gardens

❀ Setting sun garden

Create this half-circle setting sun in a sunny spot using annuals. Plant yellow pansies in the middle and alternate the sun's rays with gold and yellow marigolds.

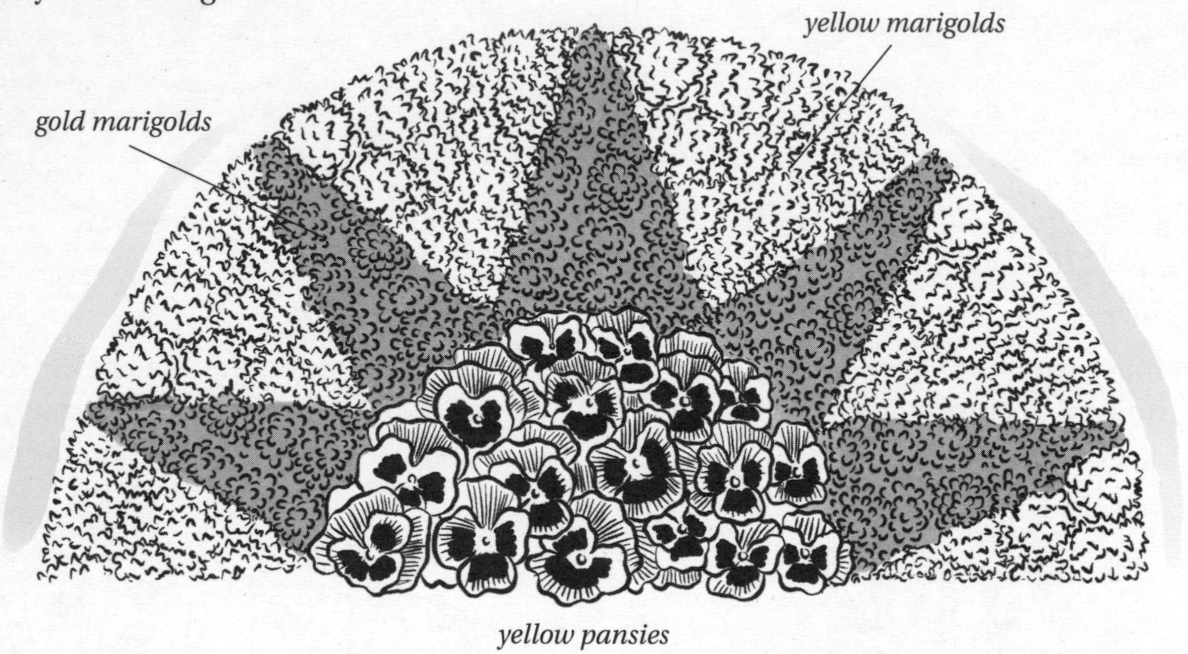

yellow marigolds

gold marigolds

yellow pansies

❀ A birthday garden

Plant a birthday garden for your family. There's a flower symbol for each month of the year.

January	carnation	July	larkspur
February	violet	August	gladiolus
March	jonquil	September	aster
April	sweet pea	October	pot marigold
May	lily-of-the-valley	November	chrysanthemum
June	rose	December	narcissus

❀ Garden of secret messages

A hundred years ago, in England, people used flowers to send personal messages. Here are some flowers and herbs and their secret meanings:

plant	message
rose	*love*
marjoram	*joy*
daisy	*hope, innocence*
violet	*faithfulness*
zinnia	*thoughts of absent friends*
lavender	*undying love*
lily-of-the-valley	*peace*
baby's breath	*pure of heart*
nasturtium	*patriotism*
ivy	*marriage*
statice	*always yours*
rosemary	*remembrance*

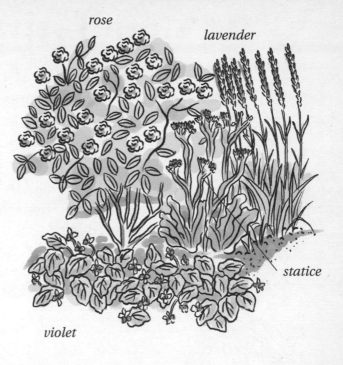

Can you figure out what secret message is growing in this garden?

❀ A plant totem garden

Native North Americans had plant totems that symbolized their special relationship with Nature. Find the plant totem that's closest to your birthday, and plant it in your garden.

March 21 to April 19	*dandelion*
April 20 to May 20	*wild clover*
May 21 to June 20	*mullein*
June 21 to July 21	*wild rose*
July 22 to August 21	*raspberry*
August 22 to September 21	*violet*
September 22 to October 22	*ivy*
October 23 to November 22	*thistle*
November 23 to December 21	*mistletoe*
December 22 to January 19	*bramble*
January 20 to February 18	*fern*
February 19 to March 20	*plantain*

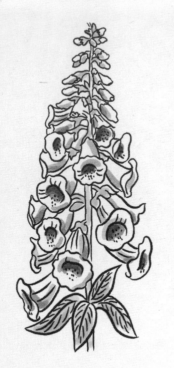

In England, foxglove grew on hills where foxes made their dens. Its flowers look like the fingers of gloves. Its other common names are "fairy-bells," "fairy thimble," "fairy cap," "fairies' gloves" and "fairies' petticoats." Picking foxglove offends the fairies, but growing it pleases them.

Fairy Garden

Many plants have long been associated with fairies. Plant some in your garden and see if you get any tiny visitors. You'll have to look in your garden at night because fairies sleep during the day. Wearing a four-leaf clover or drinking thyme tea might help you see them.

They might turn up in your garden if you plant these plants that have been sprinkled with fairy dust: oak, ash and hawthorn trees, bluebells (or cowslip), forget-me-nots, foxgloves, pansies, periwinkles, primroses, ragwort, thyme, blue vervain, wood sorrel, ferns and toadstools.

Grandma's Garden

Fill your garden with flowers that your grandmother — or even your great-grandmother — might have grown in her garden. Ask your grandmother or grandfather to help you plan and plant your garden. Here are some old-fashioned plants to try: lilac, old roses, hollyhock, delphinium, lavender, violet, bleeding heart and garden lily.

Plan for Grandma's Garden

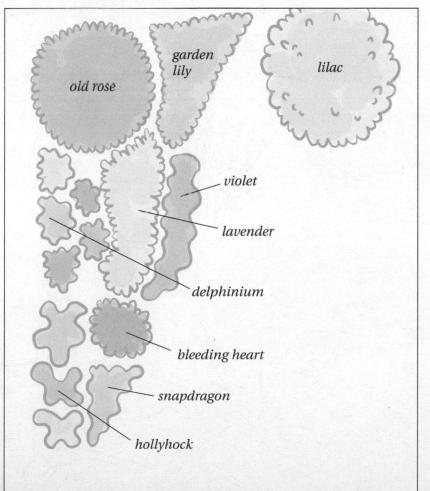

old rose

garden lily

lilac

violet

lavender

delphinium

bleeding heart

snapdragon

hollyhock

Lavender

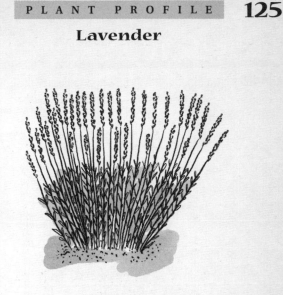

Lavender is a perennial from the Mediterranean area, so it likes a warm, sunny location with well-drained soil. The flowers are bluish purple and bloom in the summer. Some people put a sprig of lavender under their pillows to help them sleep. Its oils have been used in perfumes for thousands of years.

Gardening with Native Plants

Make some room for native North American plants in your garden. These are plants that first grew wild in North America and, over thousands of years, have adapted to the weather, soil and pests in their natural homes. Treat native plants like treasures and put them on display in your garden.

What's a Native Plant?

You can't ask a plant about its past, but that's what you need to know to tell whether it's a native plant — or an alien. Did its first ancestors grow wild in North America? Was it brought from Europe by early settlers who wanted to plant a bit of home in the New World? Or was it imported from Asia by plant breeders?

You'll find answers to these sorts of questions about native plants in seed catalogs and wildflower field guides, at your local gardening center and botanical gardens. Here are some of the terms you might run into as you're tracking down a plant's secret past.

✿ A **local native plant** is a plant that has adapted to the climate, soil and pests of a specific place or region. This is purple coneflower.

✿ A **native North American plant** is a plant that first grew wild, or originated, somewhere in North America. This is black-eyed Susan.

Purple loosestrife

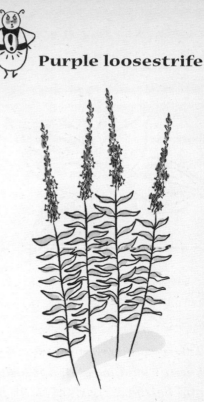

✿ An **alien plant** is a non-native plant that has been introduced or brought to an area or region from somewhere else (also called an exotic plant). This is Queen Anne's lace.

✿ A **naturalized plant** is a native or non-native plant that grows naturally in the wild (sometimes called a wildflower). Queen Anne's lace is a naturalized plant.

✿ An **invasive alien plant** is a naturalized non-native plant that has adapted so well to its new home that it crowds out native plant species. This is purple loosestrife.

Purple loosestrife is an alien plant that settlers carried to North America and planted in their gardens more than 200 years ago. Seeds escaped into wild wetlands, and the plants became naturalized.

Purple loosestrife has now invaded many North American wetlands. It takes over about 190 000 ha (almost 470 000 acres) each year, crowding out and killing native plants that some wildlife depend on for food and shelter. Terns, grebes and many other wetland birds are losing the native plants they need for their nesting sites.

Trillium

This woodland native plant is a favorite wildflower in northeast and northwest parts of North America. There are several varieties: white, purple, painted, toadshade, nodding, snow, wood and coast trilliums. The plant's name comes from a Latin word for three: the trillium has three petals, three sepals and three leaves.

Trilliums may blanket a woodland with their beauty in the spring, but that doesn't mean they spread rapidly. It takes seven years for a trillium to flower from seed. Never pick a trillium in the wild. You end up taking all its leaves and sepals, so that it has no food-making parts left. Then it dies.

Why Grow Native Plants?

Some gardeners choose native plants because they're more beautiful and fragrant than such alien or exotic favorites as pansies and petunias. Here are some other good reasons to grow a few or, even better, a collection of native plants in your garden.

✿ Local native plants like to live where you live.
Over thousands of years, plants that are native to your local area have adapted to its climate and soil. They haven't been gobbled up by pests or destroyed by disease.

✿ Local native plants don't waste water.
Local native plants have adapted to the amount of rain your area gets, so you won't have to get out the hose or watering can during a summer drought. Watering plants with a hose for just half an hour uses about 500 L (130 U.S. gallons).

✿ **Local native plants provide food and shelter for wildlife.**
Native plants need particular creatures for pollination, to sow seeds and to enrich the soil, and the creatures need particular plants for food and shelter. By growing local native plants, you're protecting plants, animals and natural habitats.

✿ **Local native plants can help save our planet.**
As wild habitats are replaced by backyard gardens that are filled with the same two or three varieties of alien plants, what you grow in your garden becomes more and more important. Grow local native plants so they don't end up on the endangered list and perhaps disappear forever. Grow a collection of different native plants to help maintain our planet's biodiversity. A healthy and balanced ecosystem needs plant diversity and variety.

Native Plants in Danger

Saving native plants from extinction is one of the best reasons for growing them on your balcony or in your backyard. The habitats of native-plant species have been destroyed by expanding suburbs and new shopping malls, by farming, forestry, pollution and invasive alien plants. People picking and digging up wildflowers are also to blame for disappearing species. So are plant nurseries that collect plants from the wild to sell to gardeners.

Plant species that need protection so they won't disappear are rated as rare, threatened or endangered (endangered is the most serious). If a plant is listed as extinct (or extirpated), it is gone forever. Some endangered species are protected by laws, and there are heavy fines for harming the plants or their habitat.

Going ...

The western white-fringed orchid is a threatened species. It lives in tall grass prairie in the U.S. midwest, but only one-tenth of tall grass prairie remains. It is pollinated by nocturnal moths and cannot be cultivated by humans.

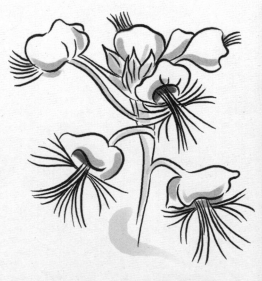

western white-fringed orchid

Going ...

Furbish's lousewort is found only in small sites in New Brunswick and Maine along the river banks of the Saint John River. It is listed as endangered. If the proposed dams for the area are constructed, its habitat may be destroyed.

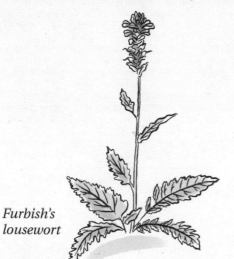

Furbish's lousewort

Gone!

The Sexton Mountain mariposa lily is now extinct. It once lived in Oregon, but its habitat was covered over by an interstate highway.

Sexton Mountain mariposa lily

How you can help endangered plants

• *Never dig up or pick plants in the wild.*

• *Don't plant invasive alien species in your garden.*

• *Write to government officials, asking for laws to protect endangered plants and natural habitats.*

• *Volunteer to help organizations that are preserving natural habitats.*

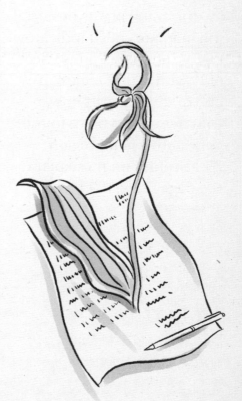

Native Plant Regions

North America is divided into seven large native plant regions, such as the Desert southwest and the Prairies. This map shows you which region your garden belongs in. The small plants beside the map are called indicator plants, and most grow wild only within that region. If one of those plants grows wild near you, you've found your native plant region. (For profiles on these plants, see pages 136–139.)

👍 **FYI**

See pages 230–232 for a list of native North American plants.

North American native plant regions

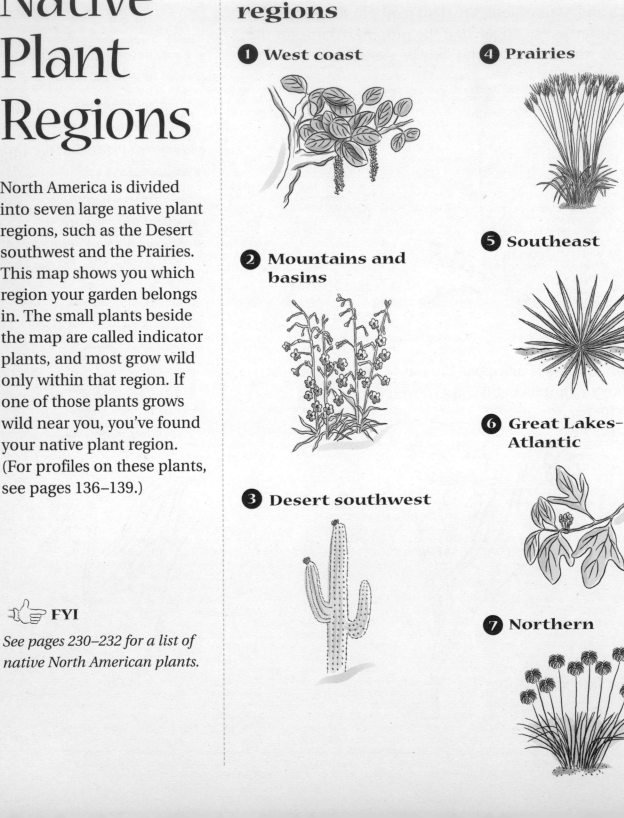

1 West coast

2 Mountains and basins

3 Desert southwest

4 Prairies

5 Southeast

6 Great Lakes-Atlantic

7 Northern

Native Plant Profiles

These are the indicator plants for the seven native plant regions in North America. Find your indicator plant and try it in your garden.

❁ West coast

Madrone (arbutus): This is a broadleaf evergreen, which means it has leaves rather than needles all year. Its reddish brown bark cracks away from the trunk in papery flakes. Its white flowers attract bees with their strong honey odor, and its bright orange-red berries, which ripen in the fall, are eaten by cedar waxwings and thrushes. It prefers rocky, well-drained soil on sites that face south along the Pacific coast.

madrone

❧ Mountains and basins

Rocky Mountain penstemon: This plant is also called beardtongue and wild snapdragon because it has fuzzy or bearded stamens that look like tongues. More than 200 species of penstemon are native to North America. This one grows on rocky slopes and in open meadows in the mountains of Colorado and New Mexico. It has bluish purple flowers in May and June. It's a good food source for birds.

Rocky Mountain penstemon

❧ Desert southwest

Saguaro cactus: This cactus is native to the Sonoran desert in Arizona. The plants grow very slowly, only 30 cm (1 ft.) in the first 25 years, and can live to be over 200 years old. The spines protect the cactus from predators, shade the stem and trap morning dew. They can store up to 7 t (8 tons) of water in their fleshy stems. These plants provide water and shelter for many animals. Gila woodpeckers, gilded flickers and elf owls live in holes right in the cactus. When its flowers bloom briefly — for 24 hours — birds, bats and insects are there to pollinate them.

saguaro cactus

✿ Prairies

Big bluestem: This native grass gets its name from the blue color of its stem. It is also called turkey foot because of the toe shape of its purple seed head. It can grow to be 1.8 m (6 ft.) tall when there's lots of rain. It is the grass in the "sea of grass" that settlers saw when they first arrived on the prairies and that fed the herds of bison. Most of this native grassland was turned into farmland, and today there's very little left.

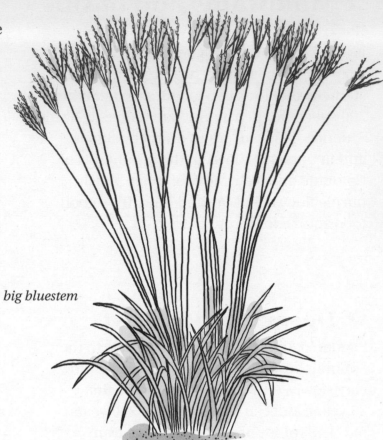

big bluestem

✿ Southeast

Saw palmetto: This slow-growing shrub is often seen poking out of a carpet of wiregrass, muhly grass or beach sunflower. It can develop into a small tree, but usually the trunk grows horizontally along the ground with its huge "armed" or "spiked" leaves growing from it like the spokes on a wheel. It has large white flowers in the spring.

saw palmetto

✿ Great Lakes–Atlantic

Sassafras: Children often call this "the mitten tree" because of the shape of its leaves. There can be several different shapes of leaves on the same tree — some with one lobe or "thumb," some with two lobes and some without lobes. A single tree can also have sections with different colored fall leaves. Its blue berries are eaten by the eastern kingbird, catbird, pileated woodpecker and phoebe. Its leaves are eaten by the spicebush swallowtail caterpillar. The bark of the root was used by native North Americans and early settlers to make a tea to treat fever. Today, sassafras tea is still used to lower blood pressure and as a herbal cure for a cold. An ingredient of sassafras, called "safrole," is used in toothpaste, chewing gum and root beer.

sassafras

✿ Northern

Cotton grass: This is a sedge rather than a grass. (Grasses have jointed stems and sedges have triangular stems near their base.) It's called cotton grass because it looks as if it has a cotton ball stuck on the tip of its stem. It grows in the wet tundra areas out of mats of sphagnum moss.

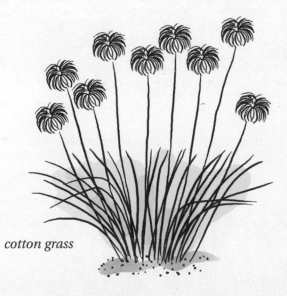

cotton grass

Native Plant Communities

Just like you, plants live in a neighborhood or community. A plant community includes all the types of plants that live together in an area and have adapted to its growing conditions. Take a walk through your neighborhood parks and green spaces, and see which plant communities live near you. This will help you choose the right native plants for your garden.

❁ A woodland community has tall trees, small trees, shrubs and low-growing plants.

❁ A wetland plant community has mostly sedges, rushes and cattails.

❀ A grassland community has small shrubs, lots of grasses and tall-growing wildflowers.

❀ A desert community has a variety of cacti and shrubs.

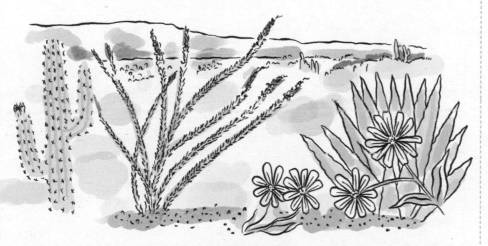

❀ Gardens are always changing

Plant communities and gardens go through a natural process of change. The natural changing of one plant community into another over hundreds of years is called succession. A pond eventually turns into a meadow. An area destroyed by fire turns into a forest again.

In a garden, weeds are the first stage of successional change. Next come sun-loving shrubs and trees and then shade-loving trees. If you don't weed your garden, it will eventually become woods. This succession process can help you create a naturalized garden, and it can also help fill in an empty garden.

Fireweed

After a fire, one of the first plants that starts growing is fireweed. It also moves into an area that has been cleared by loggers, starting the chain of succession and eventually renewing the area. It has bright, spiky pink flowers that bees love. The flowers bloom at the bottom first and then ripen into a seed with a silky wing that gets carried away by the wind.

This native plant with bright yellow flowers that bloom in the fall is often treated as a weed. Many people think it causes hayfever and other allergies. It doesn't. The real culprit is the tiny, wind-blown pollen of the ragweed plant, which often grows near goldenrod.

There are many kinds of goldenrod. The most common is Canada goldenrod, which grows in fields and along roadsides. Gray goldenrod is a smaller plant. Alpine goldenrod grows well in rocky soil, and stiff goldenrod grows in both dry and moist sites. Goldenrod is a good source of nectar for insects.

Native Plants for Your Garden

It's time for a field trip to explore native plant communities in your area. Pick the closest native plant community that has the same amount of sunlight and kind of soil as your garden. Take along a wildflower field guide to identify the plants that grow there. Make a native plant checklist for each plant you'd like to try growing in your garden.

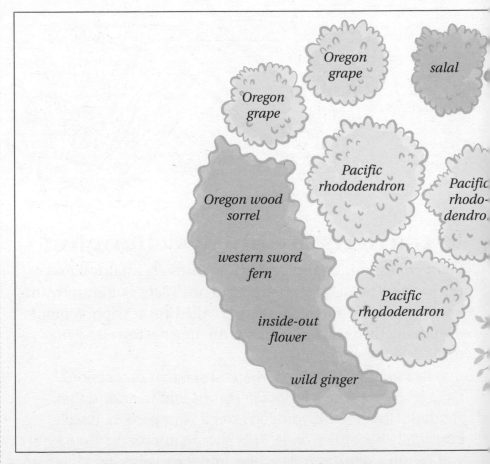

Plan for a native plant garden for the Pacific northwest

✿ Buying native plants

Check with a nursery that sells native plants to make sure its plants were grown from seed (called "nursery propagated") and not dug from the wild. Native plant societies and wildflower associations are great places to buy plants or seeds. Try to buy seeds or plants grown from seeds that have been gathered within 80 km (about 50 mi.) of your garden.

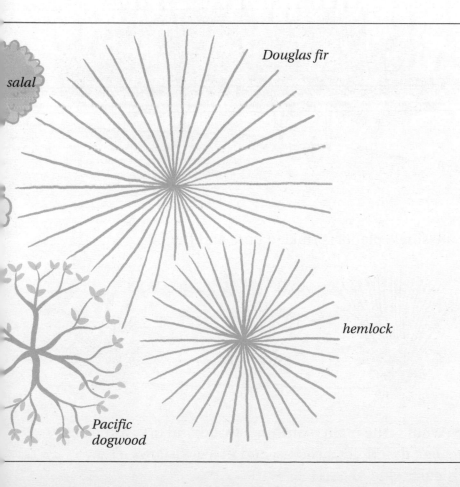

salal

Douglas fir

hemlock

Pacific
dogwood

Native plant checklist:

Here's a native plant checklist that will help you choose native plants and decide where and how to plant them.

Name of plant: _____

_____

Native plant region: _____

_____

Plant community: _____

_____

Full-grown size: _____

Flower color: _____

When seeds ripen: _____

_____

Hardiness zone: _____

Perennial ____/Annual ____

Full sun ___/ Part shade ___/

Full shade ___

Soil: sand/ loam/ clay

Water: dry/ normal/ damp

Special features: _____

_____

_____

144

Never dig up plants in the wild to grow in your garden. If you do, you could be endangering their existence in the wild. It is against the law to take plants from parks and conservation areas. It is also illegal to take plants from private property without permission. Most native plants don't survive transplanting to a different location. Digging them up usually kills them.

Imitating Nature

Nature doesn't plant in tidy, straight rows. Plants usually grow in clumps, with more plants in the middle and fewer at the edges, and shorter plants at the front and taller plants at the back.

Try creating a natural look by imitating how plants grow in the wild. Take a walk through a plant community near you and look at how Nature designs its garden.

❀ Do plants grow close together in clumps?

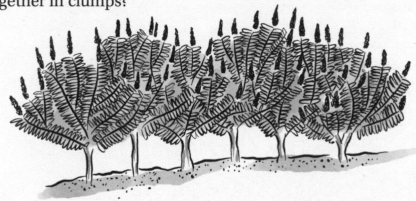

Or are single plants sprinkled here and there?

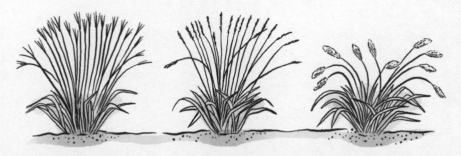

❀ What is the main plant? In a woodland, it is a species of tree; in a desert, it's a cactus; and in a grassland, it's a particular kind of grass.

❀ Do the plants grow in layers, with some plants growing over and under others? Or are some plants out in the open?

❀ Is there a variety of plant heights? Be sure to include all the levels of plants from the natural plant community in your plan. Include tall trees, small trees, shrubs and low-lying plants or ground cover.

❀ Research your plants to make sure you're not including any invasive aliens — no matter how pretty they are.

Invading ivy

Don't plant English ivy in the Pacific northwest area. It's an alien species that's invading woodlands.

Container tip

You don't want to introduce non-native plants to wilderness areas. If you're gardening at your cottage, plant local native plants or non-invasive annuals in containers, window boxes and hanging pots.

Planting Native Plants

Once you've chosen your plants, here are a few gardening tips to get them growing well.

❀ Plant the largest plants at the back first and work your way to the front with smaller plants.

❀ Water plants for a few weeks.

❀ Weed out invasive plants.

❀ A grassland garden doesn't need compost because meadow plants grow in sandy, dry soil. Mulch grassland plants with clean sand.

❀ Add lots of compost and organic matter to your garden if you're imitating a woodland site. Mulch woodland plants with chopped leaves or bark mulch.

Planting a grassland

Good spots for native plants

Turn your whole garden over to native plants or grow a few in your vegetable patch or flower bed. Native plants fit in just about anywhere.

✿ Native plants can be used where you are trying to create a natural-looking setting.

✿ Native plants can be grown side by side with non-native plants in flower beds and borders.

✿ Native plants can be grown in vegetable patches.

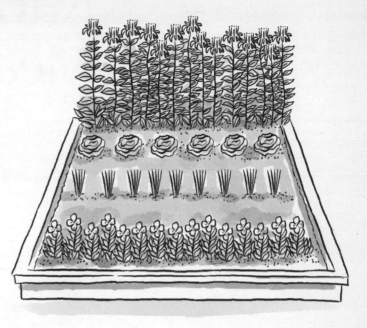

✿ Native plants can be grown in pots and containers.

Blazing star (gayfeather)

There are 40 species of this native plant that grow wild east of the Rockies. It's a tall, spiky plant with purple flowers. Blazing star likes a very sunny garden with good drainage, and it will survive a drought. Its seeds are good food for finches. It's also a good flower for drying.

Native Grassland Meadow

Plant your own prairie or grassland meadow. Include sun-loving shrubs and perennials. These plants are nice to look at, and they will attract many birds and butterflies.

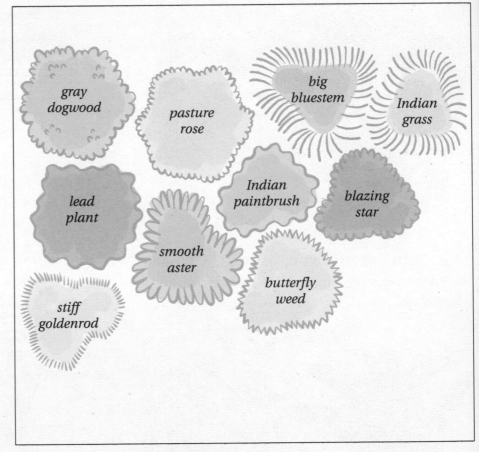

Plan for a native grassland meadow

Grassland plants will grow in poorer soil, so don't add leaf compost or any extra nutrients to your grassland garden. Rich soil makes these plants grow tall and spindly and gives weeds a head start. Mulch grassland perennials with clean sand to help control weeds.

Planting a meadow

You'll need:

- 1 gray dogwood shrub
- 1 pasture rose shrub
- 1 lead plant shrub
- 1 big bluestem
- 1 Indian grass

- 3 Indian paintbrush
- 3 blazing star
- 1 butterfly weed
- 3 smooth aster
- 3 stiff goldenrod

1 Choose a sunny site about 2.5 m (8 ft.) by 1.8 m (6 ft.) with well-drained, sandy soil. Prepare your bed.

2 Plant the shrubs at the back of your site. Plant the perennials in front of the shrubs.

3 Water the new plants for a few weeks.

Container tip

Grow a prairie on your patio or balcony. Fill a pot or two with switchgrass or Indian grasses.

This small tree has spidery yellow flowers that bloom in fall after its leaves have fallen — and when nothing else is blooming. Its seeds pop out like cannonballs when they're ripe.

Native Woodland Garden

If you have a tree in your garden, it's sometimes hard to find plants that will grow well in its shade. Imitate nature and choose plants from the woodland floor. Most bloom in spring, brightening your garden before your tree gets its leaves. If you already have trees and shrubs in your garden, you've got a head start. Just add shade-loving perennials and ferns. If you can't find some of the plants on the list, use other shade-loving natives.

Creating a woodland garden is a big project that needs a big space. Divide your plan into sections and do one or two sections a year. Find some friends to help.

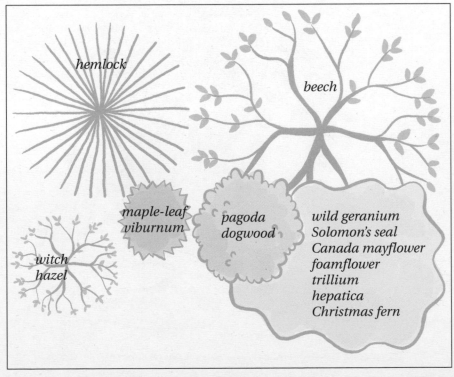

Plan for a Great Lakes–Atlantic woodland garden

Planting a woodland

You'll need:
- 1 American beech sapling (young tree)
- 1 hemlock sapling
- 1 pagoda dogwood sapling
- 1 witch hazel shrub
- 1 maple-leaf viburnum shrub
- 6 wild geranium
- 6 Solomon's seal
- 6 Canada mayflower
- 6 foamflower
- 6 trillium
- 6 hepatica
- 3 Christmas fern
- wood chip mulch

1 Choose a spot that has rich, moist soil. You'll need a site about 6 m (20 ft.) by 4.5 m (15 ft.).

2 Prepare the beds and add lots of leaf compost.

3 Plant the beech, hemlock and pagoda dogwood toward the back and sides of the site. Leave them lots of room to grow.

4 Plant shrubs in front of the trees. Plant perennials under the shade of the trees.

5 Water and mulch the plants.

Green thumb tip

After you've planted your plants, leave them alone. Their roots don't like being disturbed, nor do the microscopic creatures that live in the soil. In fall, add lots of leaf mulch, but don't dig it in. Earthworms will work it into the soil for you.

When you're collecting

- *Get the owner's or city's permission before collecting seeds from private property or public parks.*

- *No matter where you collect seeds, don't take more than a few seeds from each plant. Leave lots of seeds to produce the next generation of plants and to feed seed-eating wildlife.*

- *Never collect seeds from endangered or rare plants.*

Collecting Seeds from the Wild

Try collecting native plant seeds in your own native plant region. The seeds can be collected in the fall and planted the following spring. Seeds that look dark, dry and hard are ready to pick.

The easiest plants to grow from seed live in grassland communities. Grow asters, milkweed, black-eyed Susan, purple coneflower and native grasses in a garden plot or in pots. You can plant the seeds in the fall or store them for planting in the spring.

Collecting wildflower seeds

You'll need:
- paper bags
- wildflower field guide
- labels and a pencil
- newspaper
- tape
- plastic bags and ties or glass jars with lids

1 Carefully pull the seeds off the plant.

2 Place the seeds in a paper bag. Use a different bag for each kind of plant. Look up the plant in your field guide. Label the bag with the plant name, location and date of collection.

3 When you get the seeds home, lay them out on newspaper to dry for 2 weeks. Remove seed capsules, stems and leaves.

4 Put the seeds back in the labeled paper bags. Fold and seal with tape. To keep the seeds dry, put the paper bags inside plastic bags and tie the plastic bags, or put them in jars with lids.

5 To make seeds think they've gone through winter, store them in a refrigerator for at least 2 months. You can leave them there until you're ready to plant them in the spring.

154

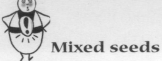
Mixed seeds

Don't buy packets of mixed wildflower seeds. They're usually full of naturalized non-native plants and annuals, which will look good in your garden only for a year. You won't know where the seeds were collected, which means they may not grow well in your garden. Instead, buy your seeds from native plant nurseries and wildflower organizations. They should be able to supply you with seeds from your area.

Native Wildflower Garden

Collect seeds from the wild and plant a native wildflower garden. Not only will you end up with beautiful flowers, but you'll also be helping protect your local native plant community.

❀ If you plant seeds from each kind of plant in a group, your garden will look like a flower bed or border.

❀ If you mix different seeds together and scatter them, your garden will have a more natural look, just like a wild meadow.

Planting a wildflower garden

Try this plan for a wildflower meadow in the Great Lakes–Atlantic region. But first take a field trip to collect the seeds.

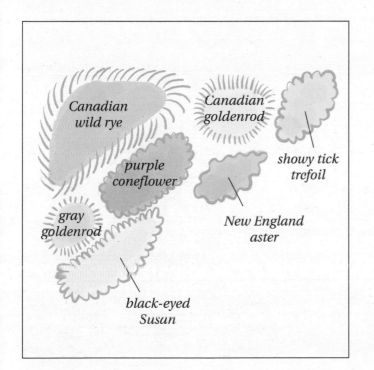

Wildflower garden plan

You'll need:
- a metal rake
- wildflower seeds collected in your area
- a watering can

1 Rake the soil flat.

2 If you want a natural look, mix all your seeds together.

3 Sprinkle the seeds on top of the soil, trying not to clump too many seeds together.

4 Pat the seeds lightly into the soil with your hands.

5 Water thoroughly and carefully with a fine spray from the watering can.

6 Water daily until the seedlings are 5 cm (2 in.) tall and then allow the soil to dry out between waterings. Continue watering for the first year until the roots are well established.

Water-Saving Garden

Watering a small lawn during summer can use as much as 37 000 L (10 000 U.S. gallons) of water. That's a lot of water going to waste. To conserve water, replace a lawnscape with a xeriscape — a water-saving garden. The word "xeriscape" comes from the Greek word "xeros," which means dry.

Lawnscape

✿ Flower beds filled with non-native plants, such as petunias, need lots of water.

✿ Some trees are thirstier than others, and the non-native Norway maple is one of the thirstiest.

Xeriscape

Here are two important ways of conserving water in your garden: take good care of your soil so that it retains water, and plant plants that can survive drought.

❀ Reduce the size of your thirsty lawn. Grow native grasses and groundcovers.

❀ Add compost to your soil and mulch around your plants.

❀ Plant native plants that have adapted to dry conditions in your area.

Prickly pear cactus

This is also called Indian fig. Before eating it, Native North Americans rubbed off the spines with a handful of grass. This cactus is often compared to Mickey Mouse because it seems to grow big ears, but they are really flat oval branches covered with spines. Prickly pear has yellow flowers that bloom for a few days after spring rain. This is a very adaptable cactus and some species grow in southern parts of Canada.

Water-saving garden plan

This is a simple xeriscape plan that will work in most regions. If you'd like to design your own water-saving garden, here are some other native plants to try:

grasses: big bluestem, grama grass, buffalo grass, reed grass, lovegrass, California fescue, little bluestem, Indian grass

flowers: lead plant, thimbleweed, artemisia, butterfly weed, fireweed, blazing star

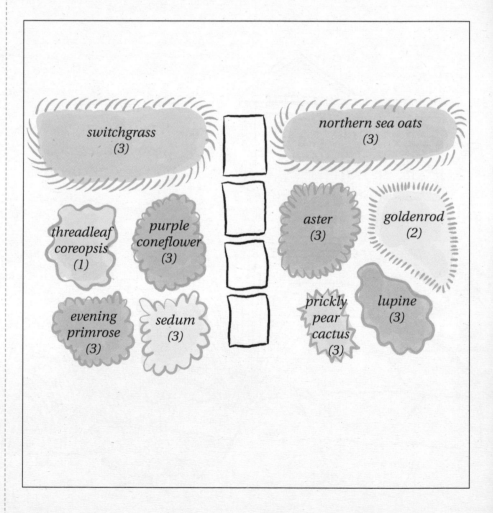

Water savers

Plants that thrive where it's hot and dry have leaves, stems and roots that are designed to hold water and to slow down evaporation. Here's a list you can use when you're looking for water-saving plants.

✿ Silver and gray leaves reflect sunlight.

✿ Leaves that are finely divided or evergreen needles have smaller surfaces so moisture won't evaporate as quickly as it does on broad leaves.

✿ Leaves that are shiny and waxy or that are covered with tiny hairs and feel like felt slow down the evaporation process.

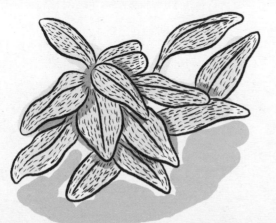

✿ Succulents, such as cacti and sedums, have thick stems and leaves for storing water.

✿ Some plants, such as the poppy, have long taproots that can reach water deeper in the soil. Other plants, such as the daylily, have fleshy taproots for storing water.

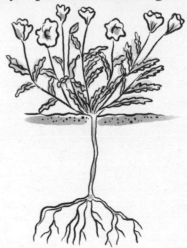

✿ Some plants, such as native grasses, stop growing in the hottest part of the summer.

✿ Some plants, such as ground phlox, creep along the ground and stay close to the moister soil.

✿ Some plants roll up their leaves to slow down evaporation.

✿ Legumes, such as the lupine, grow well in the poor soil of drier areas.

✿ Many herbs thrive in hot, sunny, sandy spots. When the sun heats these herbs, a protective haze of aromatic oil forms around them, preventing them from drying out.

Wildlife Gardens

Expect your wildlife garden to look "wild and woolly" because you're creating a home for birds, butterflies, toads and other creatures that is as close as possible to their habitat in the wild. Wildlife gardens need hiding spots, watering holes and lots of different kinds of plants — with nothing planted in tidy rows.

As you're watching your wildlife garden grow, you'll discover that a habitat made for one creature will attract others, too.

Creating a Wildlife Garden

Taking a hike through a local conservation area will show you which birds, butterflies and other creatures live in your area and what their natural habitats look like. What you see in their natural habitat is what your wildlife garden needs.

Creatures will come to your garden if you give them water to drink, places to hide from predators and bad weather, open spots for sunning themselves, and plants they like to eat or lay their eggs on.

local native plants for food

sunning spot

plants for shelter

water

shelter

Creature range

Each creature has a range or area that it lives in. If you're gardening on the west coast near the Rocky Mountains, a Steller's jay might visit. But don't expect any visits from a burrowing owl — it lives in a prairie habitat in the midwest. Find out which creatures you can expect in your area from field guides and local conservation or wildlife associations.

range of black-capped chickadee

❀ Choosing the right plants

Choose plants that match the conditions in your garden site and that will feed and shelter the kind of creatures you want to attract. Plant as many native plants as you can because that's what most creatures prefer.

Plant checklist:

Use this checklist to find the right plants for your wildlife garden.

Name of plant: _____

_____

Food for: _____

_____

_____

Shelter for: _____

_____

_____

Full-grown size: _____

Perennial _____/Annual _____

Hardiness zone: _____

Soil: sand/ loam/ clay

Full sun ___/ Part shade ___/

Full shade ___

Water: dry/ normal/ damp

Origin: native _____/

non-native _____

Special features: _____

_____

_____

How big?

The larger your garden is the more plants you can grow to feed and shelter all kinds of wildlife. But don't despair if you've only got a small space to garden in. A small garden will attract small creatures.

❀ Little spaces

If you're gardening on a patio, balcony or windowsill, grow flowering plants in pots for nectar-loving hummingbirds and butterflies. If you let your flowering plants go to seed, some seed-eating birds, such as finches and house sparrows, may also visit your windowsill. Be sure to include a dish of water.

❀ Big spaces

If you want to create a large wildlife habitat, it's best to start small. Draw a plan of your wildlife garden, then divide it into sections or different habitats and plant one or two sections each year. The larger your wildlife garden is the more carefully you'll have to plan it. Start by thinking about an edge zone.

Edge zone

The edge zone is where two different plant communities meet, such as the spot where woods meet meadow. Here the plants from both habitats mix. There's more variety in the edge zone — more different kinds of plants providing more different kinds of food and shelter. All this variety attracts more kinds of wildlife.

If there are large trees in your garden, plant shrubs and wildflowers between the trees and grass. You'll get both forest and meadow creatures coming in search of food and shelter. If you have a hedge of shrubs, let a 3 m (10 ft.) wide strip of grass beside it grow naturally for a year or two. You'll end up with an edge zone where shrubs and grass mix.

Plan for a wildlife garden

white pine

pagoda dogwood

white oak

wild grape vine

water

rock pile

switchgrass

clover

blackberry

sedge

Butterfly Gardens

Big or small, your garden can attract butterflies if you provide the right sources of food for all the stages in a butterfly's life — from egg to caterpillar (or larva) to adult butterfly. You'll need flowers that provide nectar for the adults, plants they like to lay their eggs on, plants that their young caterpillars like to eat, a source of water, shelter from cold wind and bad weather, and some sunning spots.

butterfly food

shelter

caterpillar food

water

sunning spot

Butterfly garden plan

Here's a garden plan that will attract lots of butterflies.

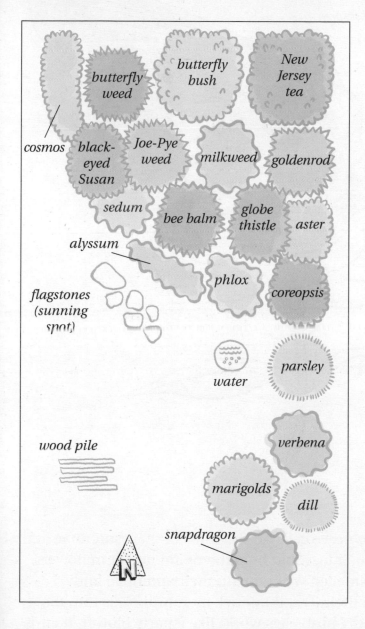

cosmos
butterfly weed
butterfly bush
New Jersey tea
black-eyed Susan
Joe-Pye weed
milkweed
goldenrod
sedum
bee balm
globe thistle
aster
alyssum
phlox
coreopsis
flagstones (sunning spot)
water
parsley
wood pile
verbena
marigolds
dill
snapdragon
N

Favorite flowers

Butterflies are always searching for sweet nectar from their favorite flowers. They are attracted to flowers by both color and scent. Here's what will bring the most butterflies to your garden:

❀ flowers with one solid color rather than mixed colors

❀ flower colors in this order: purple, yellow, blue, pink and white

❀ single flowers rather than double (frilly) flowers

❀ trumpet-shaped flowers

❀ flowers with a strong sweet smell to attract butterflies from far away

❀ flowers planted in masses or grouped together so that butterflies will notice them when they're flying overhead

❀ nectar flowers that bloom at different times to feed butterflies that arrive in your garden at different times of the year

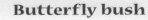

Butterfly bush

Feeding butterflies

silver-spotted skipper

This shrub attracts all kinds of butterflies. They love the nectar from its colorful flowers, which bloom in purple, pink and white. Butterfly bushes may not survive the winter in colder areas. Plant them in a very sunny, sheltered place, away from cold winter winds. In early spring, cut (prune) the old branches so that you end up with two to three buds on each branch near the plant's base. They grow new shoots very quickly, and the new shoots will have flowers.

Butterflies have nerve cells on the clubs of their antennae and on the tips of their legs that help them find nectar in flowers. Once they've "smelled" nectar with their antennae and "tasted" it with their feet, they stick their proboscis into the nectar. A butterfly proboscis works like a party blower. It curls up when butterflies are not eating and curls out when they are sucking up nectar or water.

✿ Nectar

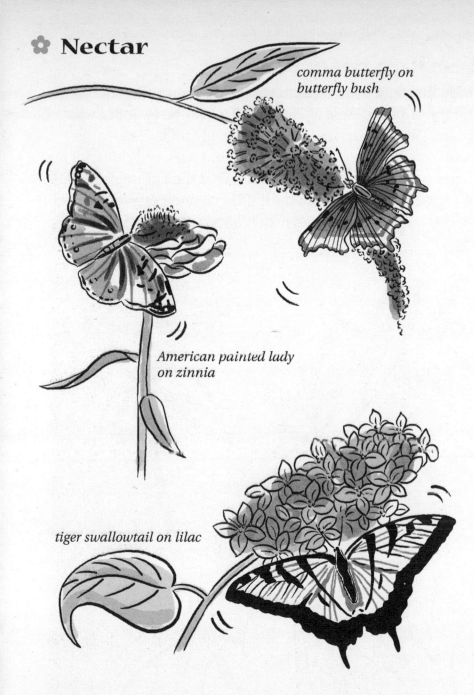

comma butterfly on butterfly bush

American painted lady on zinnia

tiger swallowtail on lilac

Butterflies prefer flat-topped flowers for easy landing and flowers in clusters so they can visit several flowers in one stop. Choose old-fashioned plants. Their scent is stronger and they produce more nectar. While butterflies are feeding on nectar, they are also cross-pollinating the flowers so the flowers will produce seeds.

Some butterflies, such as the mourning cloak, red admiral and viceroy, prefer fruit juice to nectar. You can attract these butterflies to your garden by setting out rotting fruit, such as apples or oranges, in an open spot in the garden. Add sugar or molasses to the fruit to make a really juicy butterfly treat.

👍 **FYI**

For a list of butterfly plants, see pages 233–234.

Thistles

Thistle leaves, flowers and some stems have sharp spines that protect them from being trampled and eaten by animals. But that doesn't keep other creatures away. Thistle leaves are a favorite food of the black swallowtail caterpillar. The goldfinch uses the thistle down to make a nest.

The globe thistle, bull thistle, Canada thistle and nodding thistle are wild, non-native plants. Some native thistles are Flodman's thistle, wavy-leaved thistle, yellow thistle and prairie thistle. Plant native thistles instead of the Canada thistle, which is very invasive.

Feeding caterpillars

Adult butterflies can drink nectar from many different flowers, but the butterfly larva or caterpillar is very fussy about what it eats. The monarch caterpillar eats only milkweed leaves. Swallowtail larvae prefer carrot, dill and parsley. Fritillaries lay their eggs on violets because that's what their young caterpillars like to eat. The plants that butterflies lay their eggs on to feed their caterpillars are called host plants.

black swallowtail caterpillar on leaves of Queen Anne's lace

painted lady caterpillar on thistle leaves

❀ Case of the missing Karner blue butterfly

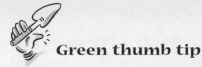

Green thumb tip

Many plants that caterpillars like to eat, such as dandelions, thistles, timothy, milkweed and nettles, are considered weeds in many gardens. If you don't want to display these weedy host plants in your front yard, grow them in your backyard.

The Karner blue butterfly is on the endangered list in the United States. It was last seen in Canada in 1991. The caterpillars need the wild lupine to eat, but this plant and its natural grassland habitat have been destroyed. Restoring these habitats so they fill up with wild lupines may attract the Karner blue back to Canada and get it off the endangered list in the United States. Plant wild lupines in an open grassy spot in your garden to help the Karner blue.

No herbicides, no pesticides

Herbicides (weed killers) will kill the plants that butterflies eat and lay their eggs on, and pesticides (insect killers) will kill the butterflies.

Butterflies, caterpillars and host plants

Butterfly	Adult Food	Caterpillar Food
Mourning cloak	butterfly bush* milkweed* New Jersey tea* dogbane*	willow* poplar* elm*
Painted lady	bee balm* Joe-Pye weed*	thistle* yarrow
Red admiral	milkweed* fireweed* fruit juice sweet pepperbush*	nettle hops
Monarch	milkweed* goldenrod*	milkweed*

Butterfly	Adult Food	Caterpillar Food
Eastern black swallowtail	phlox* milkweed* thistle*	Queen Anne's lace
Question mark	aster* sap fruit juice thistle* milkweed* sweet pepperbush*	nettles hackberry* hops
Cabbage white	aster* nasturtiums cabbage	cabbage mustard cress
Silver-spotted skipper	purple coneflower* lantana aster*	bean locust American wisteria*

An asterisk (*) means the plant is a native of North America. Choose a local native plant whenever possible. See pages 233–234 for lists of nectar and host plants.

Have you ever noticed a butterfly sitting on a flower looking as if it's sunbathing? Butterflies need to bask in the sun to get warm enough to fly. That's why you'll see butterflies flying only on sunny days. When it's cloudy, a butterfly can spend most of its day basking on the top of flowers with wide flat heads, such as Queen Anne's lace and yarrow.

Make a few basking spots in your garden by including large flat stones that absorb the sun's heat. A warm, sunny spot helps the eggs and caterpillars grow faster.

Butterfly shelters

To protect themselves from enemies, many butterflies lay their eggs where tall grasses grow. At night and during cold, rainy weather, they need roosting spots on shrubs, tall grasses or wildflowers. They also need shelter from cold winds that cool their body temperature and strong winds that make it difficult for them to fly. Trees, a hedge, a fence or a trellis with vines will block the wind, but be sure they don't block the sun from shining on some spots in your garden.

❀ Hibernating spots

You'll have to provide hibernation spots to attract these butterflies: mourning cloak, question mark, comma, angelwing and tortoise shell.

To make a hibernation spot, leave a pile of leaves or sticks in a corner of your garden. Or construct a log pile by alternating layers of logs to create open spaces between them. Leave flower stalks in your garden until late spring to protect overwintering butterflies and chrysalises.

A log pile makes a good hibernation spot for butterflies.

Water for butterflies

Butterflies can't drink from open water like most creatures. They get water from nectar and by licking it off stones or wet gravel with their proboscis. They need to be able to land and then drink without getting wet.

Fill a concrete birdbath or shallow container with stones or pebbles. Add just enough water so that the pebbles aren't covered, and set it on a pedestal or right on the ground.

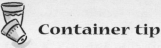

Container tip

Some butterflies are high flyers. They'll find your balcony or rooftop garden if you fill baskets, pots or half barrels with lantana, verbena, lobelia, sweet alyssum, petunias, marigolds or parsley.

Monarchs and Milkweed

The monarch is the best-known butterfly in North America. It transforms itself from a green-striped caterpillar to a gold-flecked chrysalis to a black-and-orange butterfly on just one host plant — the milkweed.

If you make room for the monarch in your garden, you'll be helping it survive as a species. The monarch is now a vulnerable, or at risk, species in North America. To save the monarch, you also have to help save the milkweed.

The monarch looks for its favorite sources of nectar — goldenrod, dogbane, Joe-Pye weed, blazing star, thistle — and the plant that will play host to its young caterpillars and their chrysalises — the milkweed. Its leaves are the caterpillar's only food source. Plant common, swamp or poke milkweed. As a substitute, try butterfly weed.

Monarch garden plan

In this monarch garden plan, you'll need a space that is 2 m x 120 cm (6 ft. x 4 ft.).

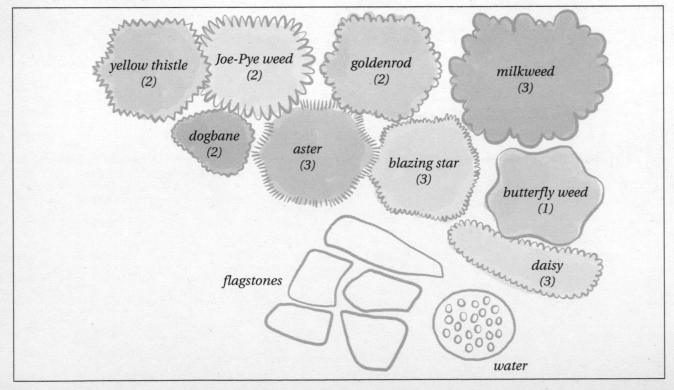

yellow thistle (2)

Joe-Pye weed (2)

goldenrod (2)

milkweed (3)

dogbane (2)

aster (3)

blazing star (3)

butterfly weed (1)

daisy (3)

flagstones

water

Marvelous milkweed

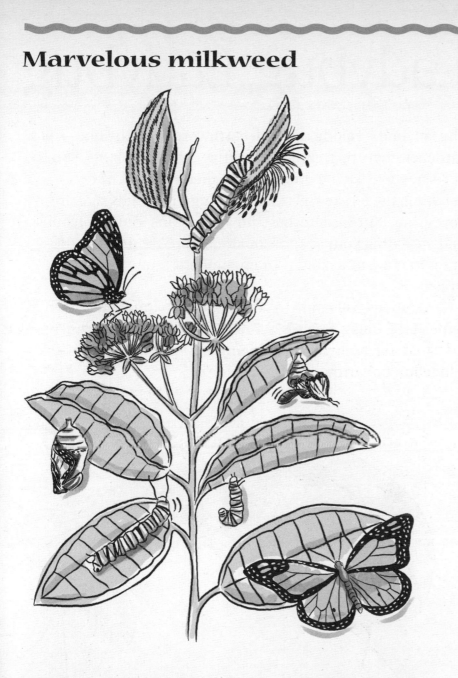

A milkweed plant has clusters of about 600 tiny, sweet-smelling flowers. It produces large green seed pods that split open in the fall so that its fluffy seeds can be carried by the wind. Start your own milkweed plants by planting seeds collected in the fall. The milkweed plant doesn't transplant well because it's almost impossible to dig up its long root in one piece.

The monarch is the only butterfly that migrates great distances just as some birds do. When migrating, it can fly 3000 km (2000 mi.) at a speed of 19 km (12 mi.) per hour, covering about 130 km (80 mi.) each day. Monarchs that summer in Canada can fly south to Mexico in about 2 weeks.

Monarchs that summer west of the Rocky Mountains fly to southern California and spend the winter in cypress and eucalyptus groves. Monarchs from the northeast and midwest regions spend the winter in the fir forests of Mexico.

Milkweed rescue

In some farming areas, milkweed may be on a noxious weed list because its leaves are poisonous to livestock. It also invades farmers' crops. Ask your local municipality to remove milkweed from noxious weed lists in urban areas where it can't do any harm to livestock or crops.

Queen Anne's lace

Queen Anne's lace belongs to the carrot family and is sometimes called wild carrot. The flat, white, composite flower is made up of hundreds of tiny white flowers, with a small red spot in the center. After it's pollinated, the flower curls up and looks like a little nest. Another common name for this plant is bird's nest. It is a naturalized alien that first grew wild in parts of Europe and Asia.

Ladybug, Ladybug

The ladybug — along with the earthworm and the bee — is a gardener's natural friend. If you grow the right plants, you'll have ladybugs laying their eggs on them. A week after hatching, the larvae will start gobbling the aphids that are devouring your rose bushes and snap beans, the mealybugs that are eating your sedums or stonecrops, and the spider mites that are attacking your cucumbers, strawberries or violets.

Ladybugs will come to your garden if you plant Queen Anne's lace, daisy, cosmos, fennel, butterfly weed, nasturtium, marigold, tansy, angelica, goldenrod, morning glory, thistle, dandelion or yarrow.

The ladybug devours aphids that devour your plants.

Garden Bees

You'll want bees in your garden to pollinate flowers, especially the flowers of your fruit and vegetable plants. Bees are so busy pollinating flowers that they won't sting you if you leave them alone.

❀ Plants for bees

Plants have developed different colors, sizes, shapes and scents to attract specific kinds of pollinators. Bees like to drink nectar from flowers that have a tube shape, such as the honeysuckle. They like blue flowers best.

Bees search for sweet nectar in the same flowers that attract butterflies. Here are some of their favorite flowers: lavender, morning glory, purple coneflower, bee balm, globe thistle, pasture rose, red clover, cucumber, basil, sunflower, catnip, aster, cleome and poppy.

❀ Powerful pollinators

Plants and their pollinators depend on each other for survival. As butterflies, bees and wasps collect nectar for food, they also collect pollen on their bodies. When the pollen rubs off on another flower of the same kind of plant, the plant is pollinated and begins producing fruit and seeds.

This perennial native plant has shaggy red, white or pink flowers. It grows 1 to 1.2 m (3 to 4 ft.) high in a sunny location. A patch of bee balm attracts lots of bees, and hummingbirds really love its tube-shaped flowers.

Bee balm is also called bergamot, monarda and Oswego tea. The Oswego people made tea from bee balm and taught European settlers how to use it.

Gardens for Birds

If you have a small garden in pots or on a windowsill, you can attract many different kinds of birds by growing the plants they need for food. If you have a larger space to garden in, you can create a home, or habitat, by growing plants that provide shelter as well as food. The more variety of plants your garden has, the more kinds of birds it will attract.

Bird habitats

Look in a field guide to find out which birds live in your area and what their habitats look like. Try to create that habitat in your garden.

The blue jay and chickadee like to live in dense thickets of shrubs and trees.

The ruby-throated hummingbird and American goldfinch live in an edge zone where trees and grasses meet.

High and low

To attract a variety of birds, choose plants of different heights. Some birds like to feed and nest up high and others down low.

Purple finches nest in treetops.

Cedar waxwings live in low tree branches and tall shrubs.

Cardinals prefer young, short shrubs or undergrowth.

Chipping sparrows like to eat on the ground.

American elderberry

The blue-black berries of this native shrub attract many birds, such as the robin, eastern bluebird and northern mockingbird. Its dense branches provide good cover and nesting sites for the gray catbird, yellow warbler, alder flycatcher and American goldfinch. It prefers moist sites and will survive in the shade. It has large white clusters of flowers in late June.

 FYI

For a list of plants for bird gardens, see pages 234–235.

Feeding the birds

Some birds, such as hawks, feed on small animals. But most birds eat berries, seeds, insects or nectar.

seed eater

insect eater

nectar eater

The shape of a bird's beak will tell you what it likes to eat.

❁ Berries

Berry-eating birds include evening grosbeaks, robins, thrushes, cedar waxwings, jays, thrashers, bluebirds, warblers and tanagers. To attract these birds, start by planting a brambleberry patch and then add a variety of trees and shrubs that produce berries at different times of the year. Try dogwood, serviceberry, pin cherry and elderberry.

Evening grosbeaks love dogwood berries.

❀ Seeds and nuts

Sparrows, juncos, buntings, finches, crossbills, blue jays, nuthatches and chickadees eat seeds from nuts, cones and seed heads of flowers, weeds and grasses. Leave seed heads in your garden to feed winter birds. Good sources of seeds include sunflowers, thistles and amaranth.

Purple coneflower

The roots of echinacea, *the botanical name for purple coneflower, are used to make herbal teas to help people fight viruses. It's also a native wildflower and much-loved food source for bumblebees, butterflies and birds. It is a flower garden favorite and grows well in dry, sunny spots.*

Many birds have adapted well to life in the city. Watch for English (or house) sparrows, starlings, barn swallows, American robins, grackles, mockingbirds, great horned owls and screech owls. In the suburbs watch for cardinals, song sparrows, northern flickers, crows, blue jays and western house finches.

Birds that stay in cities through cold winters are berry and seed eaters and insect eaters that switch to berries and seeds for the winter. Most birds that migrate eat insects and drink nectar and need to eat lots before they head south.

✿ Insects

Some birds eat insects all of the time, but most birds eat insects at least some of the time — such as young birds being raised in a nest. Insect-eating birds include the warbler, vireo, flycatcher, tufted titmouse, indigo bunting, scarlet tanager, oriole, bluebird, blue jay and woodpecker.

These plants will attract insects: goldenrod, milkweed, sunflower, clover, dill, parsley, fennel, Queen Anne's lace, daisy, yarrow, sage, thyme, lavender, catnip, dandelion, lamb's quarters and nettle.

✿ Good bugs, bad bugs

You don't have to worry about birds devouring monarchs and ladybugs in your garden. Birds won't touch monarchs because they taste terrible. Ladybugs squirt a foul-tasting juice when attacked.

Birds will eat lots of bad bugs in your fruit and vegetable garden, such as the tomato hornworm, Mexican bean beetle and cutworm. They will also eat insects that devour and destroy trees, such as the spruce budworm and tent caterpillar.

❁ Bug tips

Here are other ways you can attract bugs to feed the birds.

- Add a no-mow strip to your garden. Let a strip of your lawn grow long as a source of food and shelter for insects.

- Add some wildflowers to your garden.

- Never use insect-killing pesticides.

- If you put a small log in your garden, insects will feel at home and the birds will find them.

- If you leave a pile of leaves under shrubs or in flower beds, some insects will spend the winter there and then become food for thrushes and sparrows.

Water for birds

Provide water for birds by setting out a dish of water. Since birds also need water to cool their body temperature and clean their feathers, one of the main attractions in a bird-friendly garden is a birdbath. If you place a birdbath or dish of water under a dripping air conditioner or tap, the sound of dripping water will attract birds.

✿ Birdbaths

A birdbath can perch on a pedestal, sit on the ground or hang in a tree. It can be made of concrete, ceramic, clay, wood or stone. The sides should slope gradually to the center. It should be no deeper than 8 cm (3 in.), with a rough surface so birds can grip it with their feet.

Put the birdbath on the ground in a spot that is open and away from shrubs or trees. If it must be placed near shrubs, it should be off the ground about 1 m (3 ft.). If cats are a problem, hang a birdbath from a tree. To clean your birdbath, scrub it regularly with a brush. Add fresh water every other day.

Make a simple birdbath by placing the saucer from a clay flowerpot on an upright log or drainage tile.

Dust bath

Many birds, including sparrows and kinglets, "bathe" in dry, dusty soil to kill parasites and clean their wings. To make a dust bath, use a garden fork to break up an area of dry soil that is about 60 cm (2 ft.) square, and set bricks or rocks around the spot. Break up the soil regularly.

Cat alert!

Attach a bell to your cat's collar to warn birds that it's in the neighborhood.

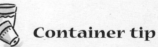 **Container tip**

Grow a small bush, such as compact inkberry or winterberry, in a large container to attract birds. To get berries you'll have to plant a male and female plant of each variety.

Birds are very fussy about nest boxes and birdhouses. Each kind of bird needs just the right size with just the right opening and just the right distance off the ground.

chickadee house

purple martin house

Shelter for birds

When you're creating a home in your garden for birds, you'll need to provide shelter from wind, rain and predators and some nesting sites.

- Snags (dead trees) are full of insects and provide roosting and nesting sites. If a dead tree in your yard isn't dangerous, do the birds a favor and leave it.

- Evergreens provide year-round shelter, as well as nesting sites and seeds.

- Some birds build their nests in cavities or holes in trees. Woodpeckers often make holes in trees that other birds move into.

- Deciduous trees and shrubs provide nesting sites, fruit and good hiding spots when they're in leaf from spring to fall.

Green thumb tips

• *Plant new trees and shrubs close together to give birds lots of hiding spots and nesting sites.*

• *Keep predators away by including plants with thorns, such as roses and hawthorns.*

• *Leave the flowers on your plants so they will produce seeds for birds, and leave your plants with seed heads in the garden over the winter.*

Nest-building supplies

• *Some birds, such as robins and phoebes, use mud to build their nests. Make a muddy spot by running the hose in an open area of soil.*

• *Dead plant stalks provide nest-building materials.*

• *Fill a mesh bag with bits of wool, grass, feathers and even dog hair. Hang it in a tree where birds can find it.*

Hummingbird Garden

This tiny bird is a special visitor to gardens, big and small. During the day, you'll see them hovering over flowers, drinking nectar with their long, skinny beaks. Anna's hummingbird needs nectar from 1000 flowers a day.

Hummingbird attractions

To attract hummingbirds to your garden, choose a sunny spot and plant nectar-rich plants with trumpet- or tube-shaped flowers. The hummingbird's favorite colors are bright red, orange and yellow.

Plant a variety of annual and perennial flowers so hummingbirds have a supply of nectar from late spring till early fall. In the southwest, hummingbirds don't migrate and need a year-round supply of nectar.

Hummingbirds also eat aphids, mosquitoes, flies and spiders. Their tiny nests are held together with spider webs. Include plants that attract these creatures, such as willow, rose, blue elderberry, pearly everlasting, aster or dandelion.

spider webs for nests

crabapple tree for shelter and nesting

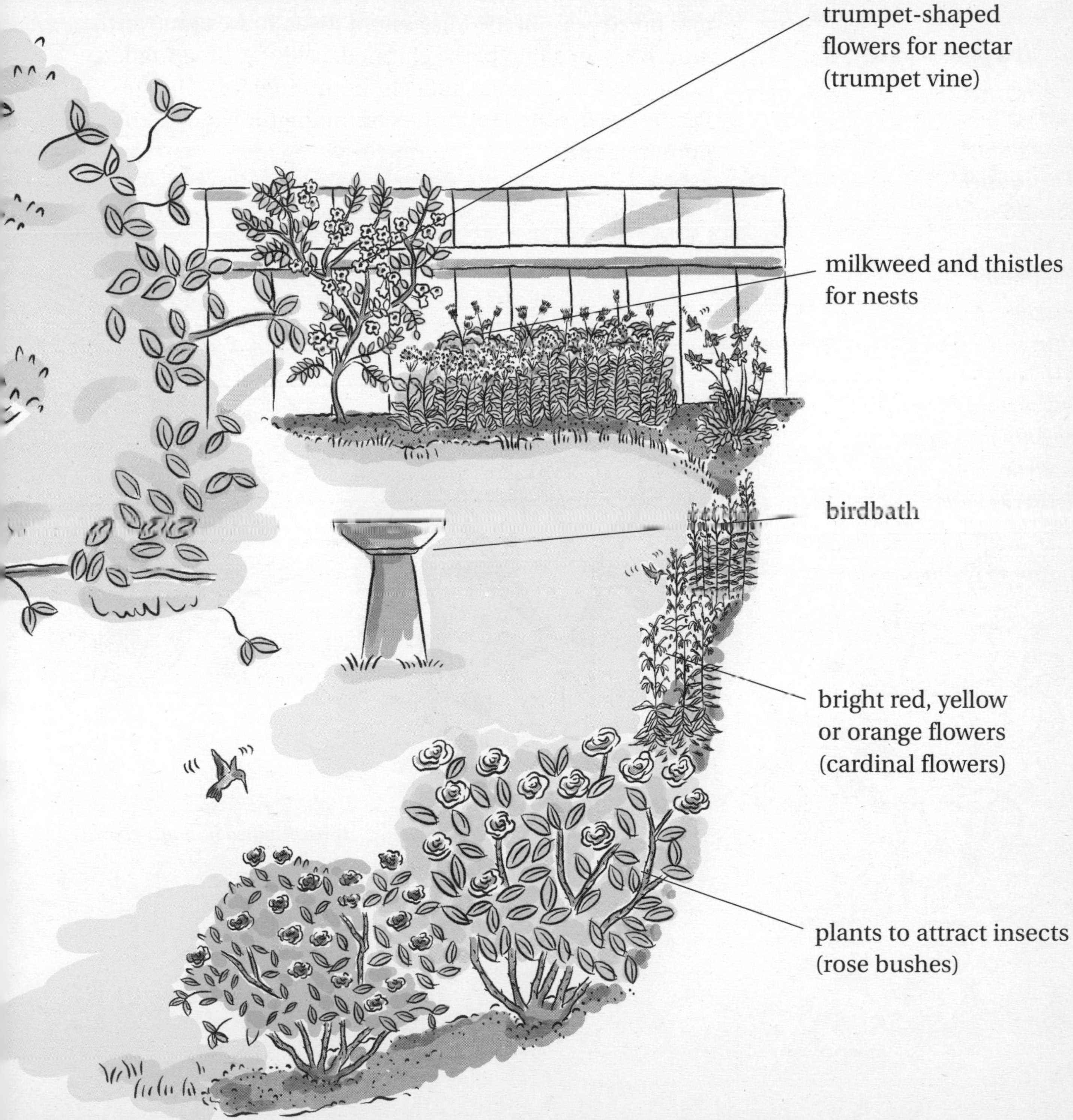

trumpet-shaped
flowers for nectar
(trumpet vine)

milkweed and thistles
for nests

birdbath

bright red, yellow
or orange flowers
(cardinal flowers)

plants to attract insects
(rose bushes)

Try some of these plants in your hummingbird garden:

butterfly bush
trumpet honeysuckle*
trumpet vine*
azalea*
chuparosa*
fairy duster*
yucca*
cardinal flower*
columbine*
foxglove
tiger lily*
bee balm*
blazing star*
swamp milkweed*
hollyhock
butterfly weed*

* An asterisk means the plant is native to North America.

Hummingbird range

The ruby-throated hummingbird is the only hummingbird that breeds east of the Mississippi River. In western North America, you'll find black-chinned, calliope, broad-tailed, Costa's, rufous and magnificent hummingbirds. On the Pacific coast, watch for Anna's hummingbird and Allen's hummingbird.

ruby-throated hummingbird

Plan for a hummingbird garden for the desert southwest

This hummingbird garden is 1.8 m x 2.5 m (6 ft. x 8 ft.)

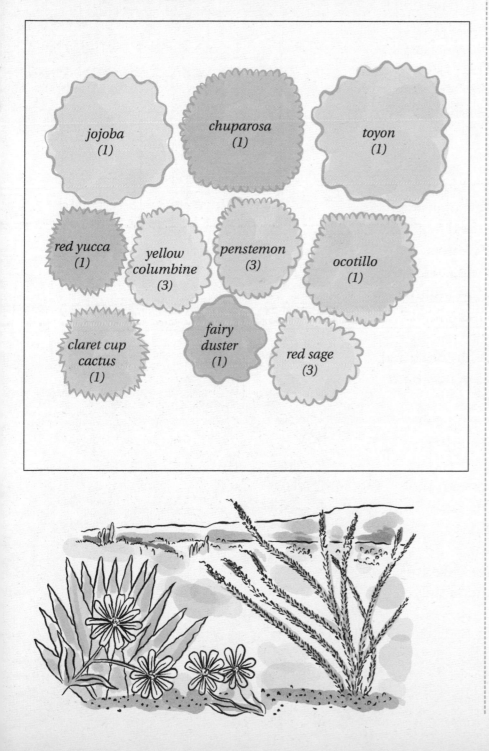

jojoba
(1)

chuparosa
(1)

toyon
(1)

red yucca
(1)

yellow
columbine
(3)

penstemon
(3)

ocotillo
(1)

claret cup
cactus
(1)

fairy
duster
(1)

red sage
(3)

Chuparosa

This is a great hummingbird shrub for the desert southwest. It is a native plant that prefers a sunny site and well-drained soil. It grows to about 1 m (3 ft.) high and 1.2 m (4 ft.) wide. In spring, summer and fall and during mild winters, it has red, tube-shaped flowers that are the favorite source of nectar for the rufous hummingbird.

Bluebird Garden

wild grape vine

Create a bluebird garden and help save the bluebird. Since the 1920s, the number of bluebirds has fallen so much that they are listed as "rare" in many areas. The eastern bluebird is in the greatest danger.

Eastern bluebird

The natural habitat of the eastern bluebird is an open space where there are lots of insects to eat. Its habitat has been destroyed to build houses, highways and shopping centers. Pesticides sprayed on farmers' crops to kill insects are destroying a favorite food source.

Eastern bluebirds are very fussy about where they nest. They build their nests in holes or cavities in trees and prefer the rotted wood of dead trees. Dead trees are now hard to find in their natural habitat.

Bluebirds have also been losing their battle with house sparrows and starlings. These very aggressive birds steal the bluebirds' nest sites and often devour their eggs or chicks.

Here's the good news: wildlife organizations have been building and installing nest boxes to help save bluebirds, and their numbers have been increasing.

elderberry

bayberry

goldenrod

daisy

yarrow

lavondor

thyme

wild rose

apple tree

Eastern bluebird range

This map shows you where and when you might see an Eastern bluebird.

1 *summer*

2 *year round*

3 *winter*

What's for lunch?

A bluebird's first choice for lunch is an insect. You've probably already got lots of delectable bugs in your garden. If you want more bugs, try planting goldenrod, dill, milkweed, sunflower, clover, parsley, fennel, Queen Anne's lace, daisy, yarrow, sage, thyme, lavender, catnip, dandelion, lamb's quarters or nettle.

Bluebirds won't eat seeds, so you'll need to grow plants with berries to feed them in the winter. Here's a list of berry plants to choose from: bayberry, American bittersweet, black cherry, chokeberry, dogwood, elderberry, hackberry, hawthorn, mulberry, wild rose, pin cherry, red cedar, serviceberry, sumac, wild grape and Virginia creeper.

Build a bluebird nest box

You may need an adult's help building this nest box. Make saving the bluebird a family project.

You'll need:
- utility knife
- 20 cm (8 in.) diameter fiber pot
- scissors
- piece of wood larger than the mouth of the fiber pot (roof)
- piece of wood about 45 cm (18 in.) long (backboard)
- hammer
- roofing nails
- a hinge with screws
- screwdriver
- hook and eye
- drill

1 With the utility knife, cut a 4 cm (1½ in.) hole that is 15 cm (6 in.) from the bottom of the fiber pot.

2 Cut the lip off one side of the pot with scissors. Position the pot against the longer board so that the lip is 10 cm (4 in.) down from the top edge, and nail the pot to the backboard in several places.

3 Screw the hinge to the center of one edge of the roof board. Set the roof board on the pot rim. Attach the roof to the backboard by screwing the hinge in place.

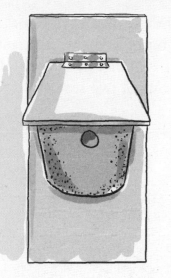

4 Screw in the hook to the underside of the roof. Screw the eye into the side of the pot, making sure that it lines up with the hook. This will keep out squirrels and raccoons and allow for cleaning.

5 With the drill, make two holes, one 4 cm (1½ in.) from the top and one 4 cm (1½ in.) from the bottom of the back board. Nail it in place through the holes to a fence post or pole that is 2 to 5 m (6 to 16 ft.) from the ground in an open area.

6 In the fall, open the lid and clean out the old nest.

Serviceberry

The serviceberry is a common small native tree or shrub that grows in most parts of North America. Its white flower blooms in early spring, and its red to purple berries are eaten by two dozen different birds, including thrushes and songbirds, as well as by squirrels, chipmunks and bears. Mule deer eat the twigs and leaves.

Bird Thicket

If you have lots of space and want to attract lots of different birds, plan and then plant a bird thicket. A thicket is many kinds of plants growing close together in a dense planting. Plant your thicket in stages, one or two sections a year.

Thicket tips

- If you have a tree and a few shrubs in your garden, add more.

- If you have all deciduous plants, add some evergreens.

- If you have just a tall tree, add plants under it.

- If you have berry bushes, add plants that produce big seed heads.

- Choose different kinds and heights of plants for diversity.

- Include some plants for food and shelter.

- Choose native plants whenever possible.

- Don't forget to add a source of water.

Plan for a bird thicket

This is a very dense thicket, with lots of plants growing close together.

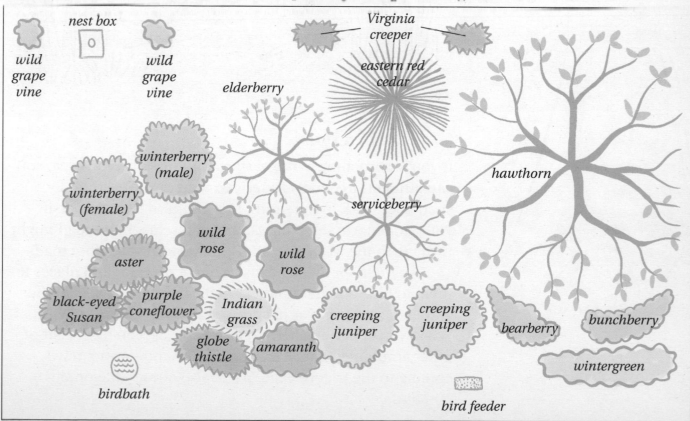

Don't take amphibians from the wild. They will try to return to their birthplace to lay eggs and will probably die on the way. You can rescue ones caught in places such as swimming pool covers and old tires. Otherwise, just wait — the local ones will find your backyard habitat.

Toad Garden

In one night, a toad can gobble 200 flies, beetles, slugs, cutworms, sow bugs or snails. Who needs bug spray when you've got a toad in the garden?

❀ Toad tips

If you're gardening in the eastern part of North America, you can attract the friendly American toad or the eastern spadefoot toad. In the south, the southern toad may visit your garden. On the prairies, the plains spadefoot toad might turn up. In the west, watch for the western spadefoot toad.

A garden for toads needs a source of water and places for them to hide and hibernate. A night-light placed low in the garden near flowers or tall grasses will attract lots of insects. When you create a garden to attract toads, you'll get a lot of other amphibians, such as frogs, salamanders and newts, coming to the water's edge. You'll also attract dragonflies and birds.

Make a toad house

Use a clay pot that's at least 20 cm (8 in.) in diameter. With a hammer, carefully knock out a big chip from the lip to make space for a door. Place it upside down on the ground in an area with plants and water.

Make a toad hole

Dig a hole 1 m by 1 m and 1 m deep (3 ft. x 3ft. x 3 ft.). Fill it with soft sand. Cover it with leaves, soil and other garden waste. This soft, sandy spot is an ideal place for toads to dig a deep hole to hibernate in for the winter.

Make a toad pond

Joe-Pye weed

soft rush

blue flag

fern

water lily

sedge

Your toad pond should get only about 4 hours of sunshine a day. If it gets too much sunlight, the pond may end up with too much algae. Place your pond in a spot where you don't mow the grass and where there are lots of plants to attract insects.

You'll need:
- a wooden half-barrel
- sand
- large rocks
- water that has sat for a few days
- water plants in clay pots with pebbles on top of the soil
- wetland plants for around the pond
- a small container of duckweed from a local pond

1 Dig a hole that is larger and deeper than your barrel. It should be about 2.5 cm (1 in.) lower than the height of the barrel. Add a 2.5 cm (1 in.) layer of sand as a base.

2 Place the barrel in the hole and fill around it with sand.

3 Place the rocks in the barrel at one side to make a ramp for amphibians to climb out and to make different water depths for plants.

4 Add the water.

5 Place two deep-water plants in their clay pots on the bottom of the barrel.

6 Place two shallow-water plants on the rocks so that the rims of the pots are just under the water. If it is too deep, put more rocks under the plant pots.

7 Pour in the duckweed. It will grow and shade the water, which reduces algae growth.

8 Plant the wetland plants around your barrel and keep them well watered. Add any remaining rocks at the edge of the pond. You should have lots of plants and a toad house nearby for shelter.

✿ Pond tips

To stop algae from taking over your pond:

- add more underwater plants (they add oxygen and compete with the algae for nutrients)
- add snails to eat the algae
- remove algae with a stick and compost it
- don't use fertilizer on your lawn because it could run into your pond

School and Community Gardens

A great place to garden might be sitting right outside your classroom. All over North America, kids are creating wildlife habitats, flower beds and vegetable patches in their schoolyards. It may take them several years, but they are transforming asphalt and grass into gardens — and living classrooms.

No room to garden at home or at school? Check out neighborhood parks and community gardens — where budding gardeners are always welcome.

Creating a Living Classroom

No matter what gets planted in your schoolyard garden, it will be a living classroom with lots of opportunities to explore nature's cycles and diversity. You and your schoolmates will also be using observing, measuring, recording and map-making skills — not to mention, having fun.

This is one garden project that you can't do on your own. You'll need help from lots of people at every stage, from raising money and making plans to planting the plants and maintaining the garden.

✿ Getting it off the ground

Start a nature or garden club in your classroom, and then invite other classes to join. Here are some things your club can do.

✿ Visit other school gardens to get ideas and advice from student gardeners.

✿ Survey, measure and make a map of the schoolyard that shows trees and other plants, paths, fences, play areas and flower beds. Locate underground pipes and cables.

✿ Find a good garden site. Poor spaces for playing make good spots for gardening.

✿ Record information about the site's soil, sunlight and rainfall. Find its plant-hardiness zone and which native plant region it's in.

✿ Brainstorm ideas about the kind of garden you want to create.

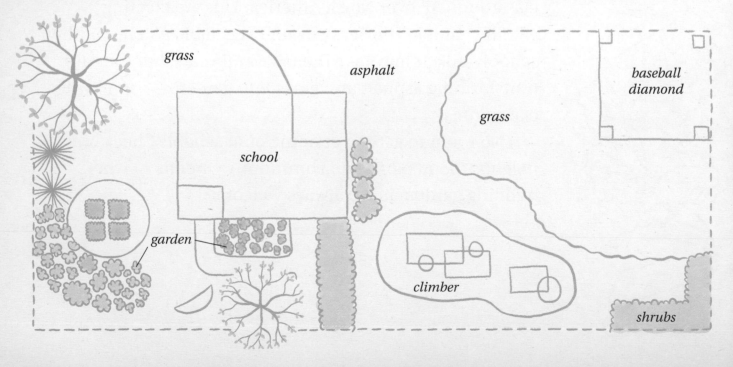

grass

asphalt

baseball diamond

grass

school

garden

climber

shrubs

Getting Started

Now that you've got a site and some garden ideas in mind, your next step is to make a plan.

✿ Making a plan

You'll need to include much more information when making a plan for a schoolyard garden than you would for a home garden. It's what you'll be using to get approval from the principal and school board, to get volunteers from other classes and the community, and to get money from funding agencies. Here's what your plan should include:

- a statement about the benefits of creating a living classroom
- a scale drawing of the garden
- a list of plants, with estimated costs
- a list of tools and other supplies, with estimated costs
- a schedule for preparing, planting and maintaining the garden
- fund-raising ideas

✿ Finding funds

You need money to start a schoolyard garden. There are seeds and plants to buy, fencing, gardening tools, and pots and other containers if you're gardening on a paved schoolyard. You and your schoolmates can raise money by organizing a fund-raising festival.

Ask your principal, teachers and school board for information about community groups, local businesses, and government and environmental agencies that will help fund school-garden projects. You may also find community groups that will help, companies that will donate garden supplies, and a neighborhood garden center that offers discounts for school-garden projects.

Designing a Schoolyard Garden

You don't need landscape architects to design your school garden. Turn the research and planning over to junior and senior classes. Here's how one school did it.

High Park Alternative School

This is a small school in Toronto, Ontario. In 1992, two classrooms planned, researched, designed and raised funds for a bird habitat on the school grounds. All the kids in the school were involved in planting a garden that transformed a hill in a parking lot into a wildlife habitat.

Plan for a bird habitat

Chloe, a grade 5 student, designed this habitat for a house sparrow.

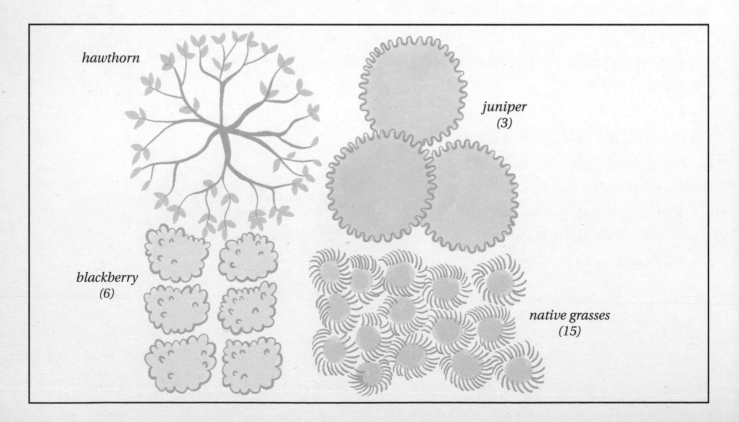

hawthorn

juniper
(3)

blackberry
(6)

native grasses
(15)

✿ Student experts

Each student joined an expert group. Each group had the help of a volunteer parent.

- The bird-expert group researched local birds and their habitats, and came up with a list of ten birds.

- The plant-expert group researched and selected plants from the native habitats of the ten birds on the list.

- The plan-drawing group made a scale drawing of the hillside plan.

- The model-building group created a scale model of the hillside bird habitat to present to the community.

- The money and media group wrote applications and proposals for funds. They also recorded all the planning and planting on videotape and wrote articles for the local newspaper.

✿ Student planning teams

Each member of an expert group was part of a planning team. Each of the ten planning teams designed one bird habitat. A bird habitat was 3 m (10 ft.) square and was planted as a small thicket with 1 small tree, 3 large shrubs, 6 small shrubs and 15 ground-cover plants or perennials.

Time Lines for School Gardens

When making your schoolyard garden plans, create a time line that shows when you should prepare the soil, order the plants, plant the plants and everything in between. Here are two time lines to get you started — one for a northern climate with warm summers and cold winters and one for a southern climate with hot summers and mild winters. Be sure to find some volunteers — either students or families in the school neighborhood — who will look after garden chores during summer holidays.

Warm summers, cold winters

September
- Harvest food crops planted the previous spring.

October
- Harvest late crops.
- Organize a harvest festival.
- Prepare garden beds for winter.

November
- Review garden successes and failures.
- Brainstorm ideas for next spring.
- Organize fund-raising.

December
- Dream about spring.

January
- Choose a garden theme.
- Draw a garden plan.

February
- Study seed catalogs.
- Make plant checklists.
- Estimate garden costs.
- Order seeds.

March
- Sow seeds indoors for long-season crops.

April
- Sow seeds indoors for short-season plants.
- Prepare garden beds and add compost.
- Plant seeds outdoors for cool-weather plants.
- Weed and water.

May
- Plant seedlings.
- Plant seeds for warm-weather plants.
- Weed and water.

June
- Harvest early crops.
- Weed and water.

July
- Weed and water.

August
- Weed and water.

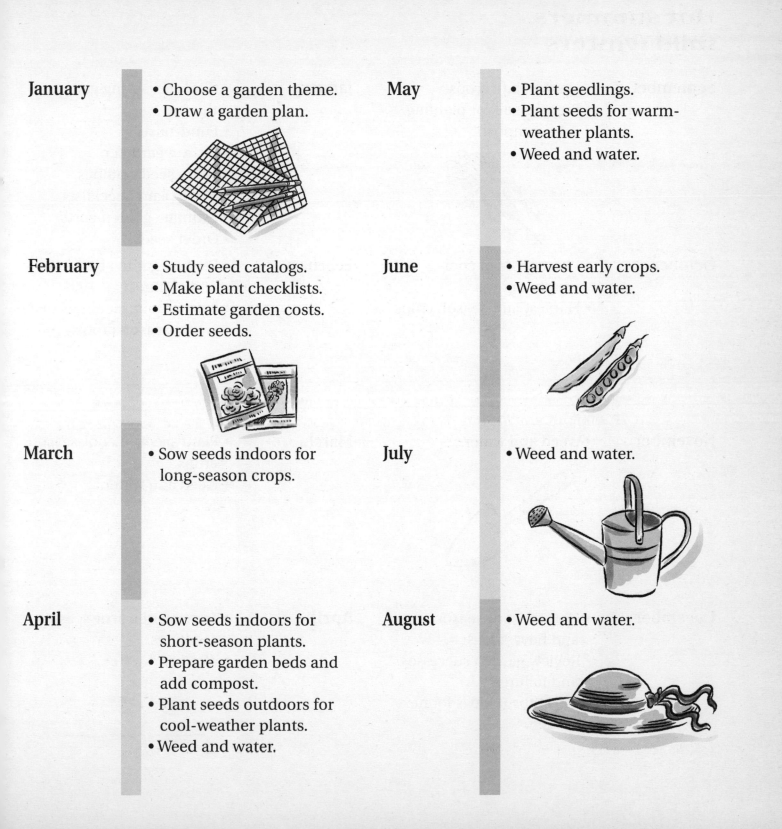

Hot summers, mild winters

September
- Harvest late crops.
- Prepare soil for planting. Add compost.

October
- Plant seeds of cool-weather crops.
- Harvest late-season crops.

November
- Weed and water.

December
- Harvest cool-season crops and have a feast.
- Review garden successes and failures.
- Brainstorm ideas for next garden.

January
- Choose a spring garden theme.
- Fund-raise.
- Draw a garden plan.
- Study seed catalogs.
- Make plant checklists.
- Estimate garden costs.
- Order seeds.

February
- Prepare garden beds and add compost.
- Start indoor seedlings of warm-season crops.

March
- Plant seeds of cool-season crops.
- Weed and water.

April
- Transplant warm-season seedlings.
- Weed and water.

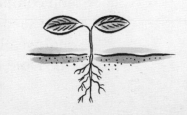

May
- Harvest early crops.
- Have a harvest festival.

June
- Harvest mid-season crops.
- Organize summer maintenance
- Select and order seeds for fall garden.

July
- Weed and water.

August
- Weed and water.

Green thumb tip

Use native trees, shrubs and herbaceous plants from the local ecosystem as a living symbol of community peace and a healthy environment.

Schoolyard Peace Garden

The kids in your school can become ambassadors for peace by joining kids around the world who are creating peace gardens in their schoolyards.

✿ International School Peace Gardens

This organization began in 1994 as a United Nations 50th anniversary program to nurture global peace through education. There are now peace gardens in 350 schoolyards in 33 countries around the world. The garden symbolizes each school's commitment to peace — peace in the school community, peace in the global community and peace with nature.

Planning a peace garden

The planning of a peace garden can be taken on by a class, a school club or just a group of interested kids.

✿   Include a inukshuk — an Inuit stone figure — by creating a rock sculpture that symbolizes peace and friendship.

- Include a bench in your garden for sitting and dreaming.

- Plan a peace pathway through the garden.

- Plan an area with wall-like plantings to create a safe, quiet spot.

- Include a birdbath or a sculpture as a peace monument.

Plan for a schoolyard peace garden

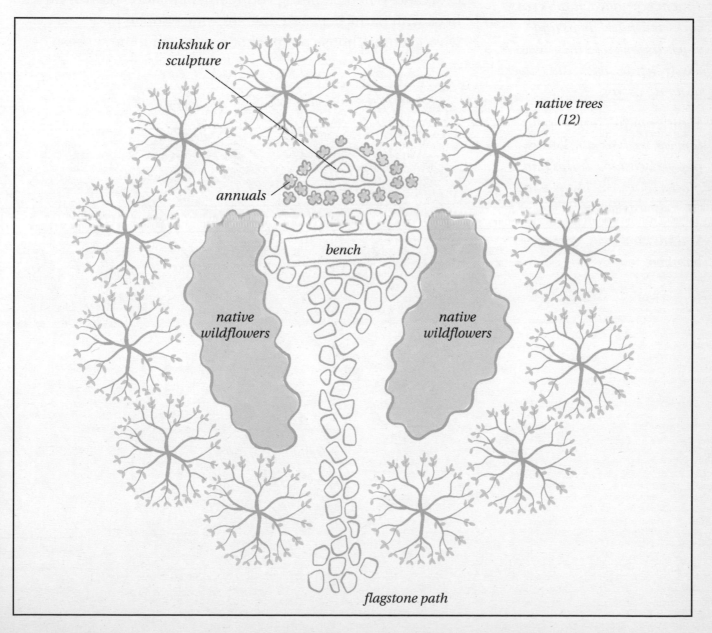

inukshuk or sculpture

native trees (12)

annuals

bench

native wildflowers

native wildflowers

flagstone path

Plants for all the senses

Smell: *mock orange, lilac, snowball viburnum, lavender, nicotiana, stock, rose, sweet woodruff, scented geranium*

Taste: *basil, coriander, nasturtium, sage, lovage*

Touch: *portulaca, lamb's ears, corkscrew hazel, hens and chickens, moss, ferns, grasses, wooly thyme, artemisia (silver mound), carrot*

Sight: *colorful, large, bright flowers, such as sunflowers, poppies, cosmos, tulips and plants that sway in the wind, such as grasses*

Sound: *pine trees, grasses, bamboo*

Special-Needs Garden

Make your school garden welcome and accessible to everyone. When planning your garden, include narrow raised beds with paths between that are wide enough for wheelchairs. Choose plants that appeal to all the senses.

Friendly features

Here are a few things you can do in your garden to ensure that all your friends feel welcome.

Raised beds

For visitors and gardeners using wheelchairs, a good height for a raised bed is 45 cm (18 in.). Wide ledges on raised beds and planters make safe seating. You can also plant in a planter box set on two sawhorses.

Wide paths

Wide garden paths and ramps instead of stairs make a garden accessible to everyone. Stones or bark on the paths allow for better traction and sure footing.

Trellises

Plants growing up trellises or walls are easy to tend.

Signs

Big, friendly signs — in several languages and in Braille — guide visitors along the paths and help them identify plants in the garden.

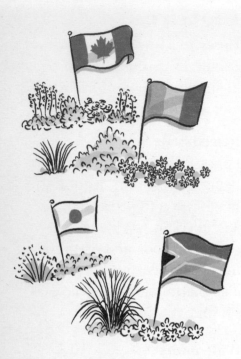

In 1992, students from Abingdon Elementary School in Arlington, Virginia, decided to create a garden that celebrated their cultural diversity. They planted three garden plots: the Old World Garden with European, Asian and African plants; the New World Garden with plants native to North and South America; and the Exchange Garden, which was started with seeds the kids collected from fruit and vegetables their families eat at home.

Other School Garden Ideas

All of the garden ideas in this book will work in a schoolyard garden. Here are some other ideas to try.

Native North American crops

Some of your favorite fruits and vegetables were first grown as crops by Native North Americans. Many were expert farmers and shared their knowledge about growing food with explorers, settlers and pioneers. Try some of these crops in a Native North American garden: corn, beans, pumpkins, garlic, Jerusalem artichokes, sweet potatoes, chilies, squash, potatoes, peanuts, tomatoes, wild rice, gourds, sunflowers and peppers.

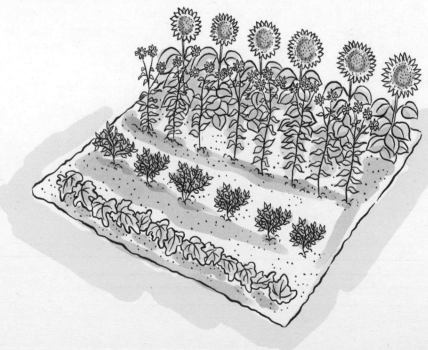

Multicultural kitchen garden

Plant a multicultural kitchen garden and grow food from all over the world right in your own schoolyard. At harvest time, organize a food festival with international dishes made from your own crops. Here are some crops to try.

For Chinese dishes:
snow peas, bok choi, winter melon
For Italian dishes:
tomatoes, eggplant, zucchini
For Mexican dishes:
pinto beans, hot peppers, corn
For African dishes:
cassava, okra, yams

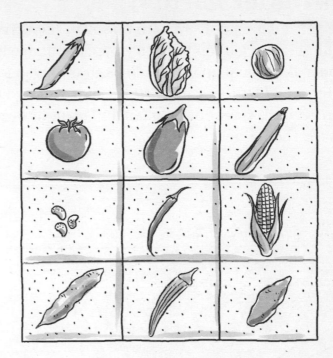

Thanksgiving harvest garden

If you plant pumpkins, Indian corn, popcorn, gourds and sunflowers in the spring, they will all be ready to harvest when you're back in school after the summer holidays.

Container garden

Have you got a schoolyard with no soil in sight? Try creating
a hummingbird garden outside your classroom with a few
big pots of cardinal flowers. Build your own wooden
planters and fill them with carrots, snap peas and tomatoes.
Try to get each classroom to plan and plant its own garden
in its own container.

Animal garden

Lots of plants share their names with animals. Here's a zoo full of plants to grow: hens and chickens, goatsbeard, cowbells, toad flax, catnip, pussy toes, lamb's ears, bee balm, dragon lilies, pussy willow, snapdragons, bird-foot violet, cockscomb.

snapdragon

bee balm

lamb's ears

pussy toes

hens and chickens

Alphabet garden

Fill an alphabetical garden using plants that have names that go from A to Z.

Community Gardens

If you can't garden at home or in your schoolyard — or you just can't get enough of gardening — join a community garden club.

Community gardens have been around since people first started farming thousands of years ago. They've included all sorts of communities and all kinds of gardens — from monastery gardens tended by a community of medieval monks to Victory Gardens tended by neighbors during World War Two.

If you're growing corn or coneflowers in your schoolyard, you're already part of a community garden. Here are other kinds of community gardens that welcome young, enthusiastic gardeners.

❀ Young and old

The Roots and Shoots program in Palo Alto, California, pairs kids in grade 3 with senior citizens. They work together in their garden, watering and weeding, learning about growing seeds, transplanting, composting, mulching and controlling garden pests. They move into the kitchen to cook what they've grown together. The seniors also visit the children's classrooms.

❁ Allotment gardens

There are beehives and compost piles right in the heart of New York City. The Clinton Community Garden was started by people in the neighborhood. They took over four vacant city lots just a few blocks from Times Square and turned them into a garden.

Allotment gardens are run as a cooperative on vacant land that is taken over by a group or leased for a small fee from the city. New lots are often distributed by lottery to people on a waiting list.

The garden of the Capital City Allotment Association in Saanich, British Columbia

❀ Botanical gardens

The Montreal Botanical Garden coordinates 75 community garden projects and several children's gardening programs. One is a farm program where students learn about caring for farm animals and growing vegetables. In the Youth Garden program, children tend their own patches of vegetables, herbs and flowers 2 half-days a week. During the summer Nature Day Camp, children work in their garden plots every morning and spend their afternoons doing natural science activities.

✿ Kids clubs

If you join Boy Scouts or Girl Scouts of America, Scouts Canada or Girl Guides of Canada, you can garden and earn gardening badges. In rural areas, many 4-H Clubs have garden programs.

The 4-H Children's Garden at Michigan State University has 56 theme gardens, including the Wizard of Oz garden, the Secret Garden, the Alice in Wonderland Maze, which is enclosed with a cedar hedge, and the Dinosaur Garden with plants that once shared the land with dinosaurs.

Neighborhood Gardening

❁ Neighborhood parks

Get involved with gardening projects right in your own neighborhood. In many cities and towns, groups of volunteer gardeners are cleaning up neighborhood parks and planting trees. Other groups focus on protecting local habitats and planting native plants.

Children planting native plant seedlings in a park.

❀ "You Gotta Have Park"

Prospect Park is a naturalized park that provides an urban oasis in Brooklyn, New York. On "You Gotta Have Park" days, a volunteer group called Volunteers in Prospect Park picks up litter, plants seedlings and raises money for the park. School groups plant trees on Arbor Day. The Scouts have adopted a section of the park to clean up and plant. High school students in the neighborhood build wooden cribs on hillsides to help stop erosion. Children's groups transplant native-plant seedlings that are grown in the greenhouse.

❀ Park stewards

The High Park Volunteer Stewardship Program is a group of 200 volunteers working to restore the ecosystems in High Park, a 160-ha (399-acre) park in Toronto, Ontario. Volunteers of all ages harvest seeds, propagate seeds, plant seedlings, remove invasive weeds and conduct plant rescues. Their main focus is the restoration of native-plant species in the park, but they also help local schools and children's groups plant native plants.

Children building wooden cribs to stop erosion.

❀ Wildlife jigsaw garden

Some city gardening groups create wildlife corridors — places where animals can travel safely from one area to another — in their neighborhoods. Each neighbor becomes one piece in the wildlife jigsaw garden by planting trees in a corner, a shrubby hedgerow and a meadow area with native wildflowers and grasses. When they're all pieced together, the neighborhood has a healthy ecosystem for plants and animals — and lovely gardens in its backyards.

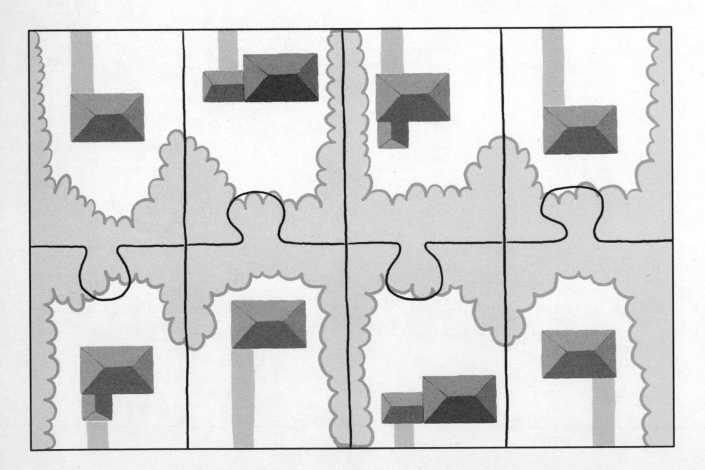

✿ Be a good neighbor

When planning your garden, remember that you are part of a neighborhood ecosystem. Keep in mind how your garden will affect the plants, animals and neighbors around you.

- Spread the word about your garden. The more you explain it to your neighbors, the more they will appreciate your efforts and they may even start gardening, too.

- If you are making a wildlife garden with native plants, explain your plans to your neighbors. Maybe they will plant native species, too.

- Animals ignore property lines, so the more animal-friendly plants there are in other gardens the more animals will be attracted to yours.

- If you're gardening close to a ravine, wetland, park or a protected area, research your plant choices carefully. Don't plant harmful or invasive species.

- If there's farmland next door to your garden, don't plant species that could harm crops or livestock.

- If your neighbor is a gardener, you'll have lots of fun exchanging gardening tips over the fence.

Plant Lists

Native Plants

Here's a list of some common native plants that grow in different plant communities in each of the native plant regions.

WEST COAST

❀ Coastal

Trees and shrubs: giant fir, big-leaf maple, madrone, California sage, coyote bush, monkey flower, coffeeberry, red elderberry, manzanita, California wax myrtle

Herbaceous plants: sea pink, lizard's tail, California poppy, Douglas iris, lupine, blue-eyed grass, California fescue

❀ California Oak Savannah

Trees and shrubs: coffeeberry, Monterey manzanita, toyon, live oak

Herbaceous plants: reedgrass, California oatgrass, lupine, gilia, California poppy

❀ Douglas Fir Woodland

Tree and shrubs: Douglas fir, vine maple, big-leaf maple, Pacific madrone, Pacific dogwood, Oregon grape, red huckleberry, salal

Herbaceous plants: western sword fern, Oregon wood sorrel, inside-out flower

❀ Garry Oak Prairie

Trees and shrubs: Garry oak, California black oak, Ponderosa pine, Pacific madrone, Oregon grape, shrubby cinquefoil

Herbaceous plants: Columbia lily, nodding onion, saxifrage, coastal strawberry, lupine

MOUNTAINS AND BASINS

❀ Mountain Meadow

Trees and shrubs: booth willow, Geyer willow, peach-leaved willow, western azalea

Herbaceous plants: alpine bluegrass, alpine milkvetch, cliff sedge, gilia, paintbrush, Rocky Mountain penstemon, Rocky Mountain iris, silver sedge

❀ Great Basin Sagebrush Desert

Trees and shrubs: big sagebrush, gooseberry, rabbitbrush, low sagebrush, Mormon tea

Herbaceous plants: blanketflower, blue grama, buckwheat, desert paintbrush, goldenrod, Indian rice grass, scarlet gilia

❀ Pinyon–Juniper Woodland

Trees and shrubs: Rocky Mountain juniper, Utah juniper, pinyon pine, Ponderosa pine, western serviceberry

Herbaceous plants: blue grama, buckwheat, hairy golden aster, prairie sunflower, wild four o'clock

❀ Aspen Forest

Trees and shrubs: alder, narrowleaf cottonwood, common juniper, quaking aspen

Herbaceous plants: blue columbine, bluegrass, bracken fern, silver lupine, wild strawberry

DESERT SOUTHWEST

❀ Sonoran Cactus Desert

Trees and shrubs: blue palo verde, creosote bush, velvet mesquite, brittlebush, fairy duster

Herbaceous plants: buffalo grass, desert marigold, penstemon, desert zinnia, evening primrose

Cacti: barrel, ocotillo, organ-pipe, claret cup cactus, saguaro, yucca, New Mexico agave

❀ Chihuahuan Desert

Shrubs: crcosote bush, century plant, desert willow, mesquite, ocotillo, chamisa, Apache plume

Herbaceous plants: Texas sage, desert zinnia, blackfoot daisy, giant four o'clock, penstemon, sand love grass

❀ Semi-Desert Grassland:

Trees and shrubs: juniper, creosote bush, acacia, mesquite

Herbaceous plants: black grama, slender grama, tobosa grass, desert marigold, penstemon, tickseed

❀ Short Grass Prairie

Trees and shrubs: rabbitbrush, Rocky Mountain juniper, prickly pear cactus

Herbaceous plants: buffalo grass, blue grama, buffalo gourd, Rocky Mountain bee plant, yucca

❀ Mixed Grass Prairie

Trees and shrubs: willow, cottonwood, ash

Herbaceous plants: little bluestem, threadleaf sedge, side-oats grama, buffalo grass, blue grama, purple prairie clover

❀ Tall Grass Prairie

Trees and shrubs: cottonwood, green ash, American elm, bur oak, pasture rose, gray dogwood, aspen, lead plant

Herbaceous plants: big bluestem, Indian grass, blazing star, prairie coreopsis, compass plant, purple prairie clover, milkweed, butterfly weed, goldenrod, aster, Indian paintbrush, dogbane

SOUTHEAST

❀ Seaside Sand Dune

Trees and shrubs: wax myrtle, bayberry, yucca

Herbaceous plants: American beach grass, sea oats, Cape beach grass, blanketflower

❀ Pine–Oak Forest

Trees and shrubs: loblolly pine, shortleaf pine, longleaf pine, blackjack oak, live oak, magnolia, redbud, bayberry, persimmon, fetterbush, flowering dogwood, hawthorn

Herbaceous plants: beautyberry, Carolina jessamine, panic grass, little bluestem, switchgrass

❀ **Floodplain**

Trees and shrubs: Carolina ash, bald cypress, black willow, box elder, buttonbush, persimmon, water hickory, red maple, swamp chestnut oak

Herbaceous plants: wisteria, Dutchman's breeches, giant cane, Spanish moss, trout lily

GREAT LAKES–ATLANTIC

❀ Coastal

Trees and shrubs: post oak, pitch pine, sand rose, bearberry, bayberry, poison ivy, inkberry

Herbaceous plants: beach heather, seaside goldenrod, seaside spurge, beach pea, beachgrass, sea oats

❀ Northern Hardwood Forest

Trees and shrubs: sugar maple, beech, yellow birch, black cherry, white ash, red oak, hemlock, white pine, striped maple, mountain laurel

Herbaceous plants: painted trillium, wood sorrel, pink lady's slipper, wood lily, spotted wintergreen, wild sarsaparilla

❀ Maple–Beech Forest

Trees and shrubs: American beech, sugar maple, tulip tree, flowering dogwood, witch hazel, spicebush, pagoda dogwood

Herbaceous plants: wild geranium, Solomon's seal, Canada mayflower, foamflower, trillium, hepatica, Christmas fern

❀ Pine-Oak Forest

Trees and shrubs: pitch pine, white pine, black oak, white oak, red oak, inkberry, blueberry

Herbaceous plants: blue-eyed grass, butterfly weed, blazing star, hawkweed, poverty oat grass

❀ Great Lakes Mixed Forest

Trees and shrubs: beech, eastern hemlock, white pine, red pine, white cedar, red and sugar maples, red oak, white ash, dogwood, elderberry

Herbaceous plants: bluebead lily, Canada mayflower, false Solomon's seal, trillium

❀ Grassy Meadow

Trees and shrubs: sumac, blueberry, blackberry, red cedar, sassafras, hawthorn

Herbaceous plants: little bluestem, Indian grass, switchgrass, big bluestem, broomsedge, goldenrod, aster, pussy toes, butterfly weed, black-eyed Susan, milkweed, thistle

NORTHERN

❀ Boreal

Trees and shrubs: black spruce, white spruce, balsam fir, tamarack, Saskatoon berry, bog willow, Labrador tea, bearberry, creeping juniper, blueberry

Herbaceous plants: sphagnum moss, old man's beard lichen, reindeer moss, wintergreen, cotton grass

❀ Arctic Tundra

Dwarf trees and shrubs: dwarf willow, birch, Labrador tea, blueberry

Herbaceous plants: sphagnum moss, sedge, willow herb, lichen, cotton grass, Arctic white heather, purple saxifrage, mountain avens

Plants That Attract Butterflies

Here's a list of native plants that will attract a variety of butterflies.

WEST COAST

Trees and shrubs: California lilac, toyon, blue elderberry, evergreen huckleberry, California buckeye, coast live oak, New Jersey tea

Herbaceous plants: Douglas iris, tiger lily, lupine, scarlet monkey flower, wild buckwheat, western wallflower, gilia, evening primrose, California coneflower, senna, milkweed, deer grass, goldenrod, Joe-Pye weed, bee balm

MOUNTAIN AND BASINS

Trees and shrubs: rabbitbrush, gambel oak, narrowleaf cottonwood

Herbaceous plants: wild white yarrow, blanket flower, showy goldeneye, lead plant, butterfly weed, red valerian, gayfeather

DESERT SOUTHWEST

Trees and shrubs: claret cup cactus, pink fairy duster, brittlebush, rabbitbrush, ocotillo, chuparosa, littleleaf sumac, acacia, blue palo verde, desert willow, honey mesquite, Joshua tree

Herbaceous plants: desert marigold, Parry's penstemon, New Mexico agave, blackfoot daisy, milkweed, aster, chia sage

PRAIRIES

Trees and shrubs: soapweed yucca, common hackberry, downy hawthorn, eastern cottonwood, New Jersey tea

Herbaceous plants: pearly everlasting, butterfly weed, purple coneflower, Maximillan sunflower, dotted gayfeather, wild bergamot, goldenrod, aster

SOUTHEAST

Trees and shrubs: hoary azalea, pawpaw, sugarberry hackberry, flowering dogwood, American holly, tulip tree, trumpet honeysuckle

Herbaceous plants: Joe-Pye weed, cardinal flower, phlox, butterfly weed, gayfeather

GREAT LAKES–ATLANTIC

Trees and shrubs: spicebush, American cranberry bush, eastern redbud, pin cherry, sassafras, wild grape

Herbaceous plants: wild columbine, New England aster, bee balm, black-eyed Susan, purple coneflower, milkweed, butterfly weed, goldenrod, Joe-Pye weed

✿ Host Plants

Here's a list of plants that host a variety of caterpillars. An asterisk (*) means that the plant is native to North America.

Trees: aspen*, willow*, alder*, birch*, wild cherry*, poplar*, hackberry*, elm*

Shrubs: dogwood*, sumac*, buckthorn*, gooseberry*, blackberry*, blueberry*, lilac, spicebush*, viburnum*, fairy duster*

Perennials: butterfly-weed*, milkweed*, parsley, plantain, thistle*, Queen Anne's lace, aster*, clover, viper's bugloss, nettle, lupine*, violet*, dandelion, grasses*, sheep sorrel, dock

Annuals: nasturtium, marigold, sweet peas, snapdragon, pansy, alyssum, hollyhock

Vegetables: bean, cabbage, broccoli, carrot, parsnip

Herbs: dill, parsley, fennel, lavender

Plants That Attract Birds

These native plants will attract a variety of birds.

WEST COAST

Tall trees: madrone, rocky mountain fir, Douglas fir, western hemlock, coast live oak

Small trees: mountain dogwood, California live oak, toyon

Large shrubs: California lilac, red elder, ninebark, wax myrtle, manzanita, California coffeeberry, red-flowering currant, golden currant, thimbleberry, evergreen huckleberry

Small shrubs: Oregon grape, sage

Ground covers: manzanita, salal

MOUNTAINS AND BASINS

Tall trees: Englemann spruce, Ponderosa pine, Colorado spruce

Small trees: hawthorn, Rocky Mountain juniper, pinyon pine, gambel oak, quaking aspen, narrowleaf cottonwood

Large shrubs: butterfly bush, wolfberry, serviceberry

Small shrubs: golden currant, western thimbleberry, banana yucca

Vines: trumpet honeysuckle, riverbank grape

Ground covers: bunchberry, coralbells, wild strawberry, side-oats grama, creeping mahonia

DESERT SOUTHWEST

Small trees: acacia, blue palo verde, mesquite, Joshua tree, netleaf hackberry, Mexican redbud, desert willow, cottonwood

Large shrubs: red barberry, ocotillo, littleleaf sumac, creosote bush, desert hackberry, wolfberry

Small shrubs: pink fairy duster, brittlebush, chuparosa, Mormon tea, red sage, manzanita, creosote bush, coyote willow

Ground covers: desert marigold, bush muhly, deer grass, thistle, wild sunflower, penstemon

Cacti: prickly pear, saguaro, cholla, agave, ocotillo

PRAIRIES

Tall trees: eastern cottonwood, bur oak, green ash

Small trees: cockspur and downy hawthorn, hackberry, red cedar

Large shrubs: gray dogwood, desert willow, red-flowering currant, ocotillo, smooth sumac, serviceberry

Small shrubs: coralberry, western snowberry, prairie rose

Ground covers: creeping juniper, little bluestem, lowbush blueberry, big bluestem, blue grama, purple coneflower, Maximillan sunflower

SOUTHEAST

Tall trees: southern live oak, American sweetgum, shagbark hickory, sugar hackberry, longleaf pine, loblolly pine, red cedar

Small trees: American holly, black cherry, black tupelo, common persimmon, dwarf chinquapin oak, red buckeye, sassafras, flowering dogwood, eastern red cedar, red mulberry, southern live oak

Large shrubs: arrowood viburnum, possumhaw, dahoon holly, magnolia

Small shrubs: inkberry, winterberry

Vines: trumpet honeysuckle, trumpet vine

Ground covers: common juniper, wintergreen, beach sunflower, purple muhly grass

GREAT LAKES–ATLANTIC

Tall trees: red pine, white pine, white spruce, white, red and black oaks, hackberry, eastern hemlock, American beech, black cherry, sugar maple

Small trees: hawthorn, mountain ash, eastern white cedar, eastern red cedar, flowering dogwood, red mulberry, paper birch, gray birch, Allegheny serviceberry, pin cherry, sassafras, hemlock

Large shrubs: serviceberry, sumac, dogwood, elderberry, viburnum, spicebush, highbush blueberry, Canada yew, common juniper

Low shrubs: creeping juniper, bayberry, wild rose, horizontal red cedar, inkberry, winterberry, snowberry, blueberry

Vines: American bittersweet, Virginia creeper, wild grape

Ground covers: bearberry, bunchberry, partridgeberry, wintergreen, wild strawberry

❀ Seedy Plants

Here's a list of flowering plants and grasses that produce seeds that birds like to eat. An asterisk (*) means the plant is native to North America.

Perennials: aster*, purple coneflower*, black-eyed Susan*, bee balm*, columbine*, coreopsis*, amaranth, blanket flower*, yarrow, goldenrod*, globe thistle, wild geranium*, oxeye daisy

Grasses and "weeds": big and little bluestem*, Indian grass*, knotweed, panic grass*, sheep sorrel, lamb's quarters, crabgrass, pigweed, chickweed

Annuals: sunflower*, cosmos, verbena*, four o'clock*, phlox*, California poppy*, cornflower, zinnia, larkspur, love-in-a-mist, marigold

❀ Berry Plants

Here are some berry-bearing plants that will attract birds. An asterisk (*) means the plant is native to North America.

Trees: mountain ash, sumac*, black or pin cherry*, crabapple, red cedar*, red mulberry*, hackberry*, hawthorn*, sassafras*

Shrubs: elderberry*, rose*, serviceberry*, bayberry*, blackberry*, raspberry*, blueberry*, black currant*, winterberry*, Oregon grape*, common juniper*, firethorn, viburnum*, dogwood*

Vines: American bittersweet*, wild grape*, Virginia creeper*

Ground covers: bearberry*, bunchberry*, cotoneaster, creeping juniper*

Index

A

Alien plant, 129, 130, 132, 145
Allium, 101
Allotment gardens, 223
Alyssum, 167
Amaranth, 199
American beech, 150, 151
American elderberry, 182
American goldfinch, 180
American painted lady butterfly, 169
Amphibians, 200–203
Annuals, 22, 94, 95, 96, 215
Apple tree, 194, 195
Arbutus, 136
Aster, 148, 149, 155, 158, 167, 176, 199
Azalea, 108

B

Baby's breath, 112, 123
Basil, 76, 77, 78, 79, 90, 91, 216
Bayberry, 194, 195
Beans, 46, 60, 61, 62, 63, 80–81, 90, 91, 218, 219
Bearberry, 199
Bee balm, 167, 179, 221
Bees, 108, 178, 179
Bellflower, 116
Big bluestem, 138, 148, 149
Birds:
    birdbaths, 187
    city birds, 184
    dust bath, 187
    Eastern bluebird, 194–197
    feeding, 82, 182–185, 192, 196, 199
    garden plans, 193, 199
    habitats, 180
    hummingbirds, 190–193
    nests, 188, 189, 196, 197
    plants that attract, 181, 182, 183, 188, 190, 199, 192, 196, 234–235
    shelter, 188–189
    thicket, 198, 199
    water, 186

Black swallowtail butterfly, 170
Black-eyed Susan, 98, 128, 155, 167, 199
Blackberry, 165, 208
Blazing star, 148, 149, 176
Bleeding heart, 99, 125
Blue flag, 202
Blue jay, 180
Bluebird. *See* Eastern bluebird
Botanical gardens, 224
Botanical name, 22
Bouquets, 106–107
Brambles, 84–85. *See also* Blackberry
Bulbs, 100–101
Bunchberry, 199
Butterflies:
    basking, 174
    caterpillars, 170, 171, 172–173
    feeding, 168, 169, 172–173
    garden plans, 167
    hibernating, 174
    Karner blue, 171
    monarch, 176–177
    shelter, 174
    water, 174
    flowers that attract, 104, 167, 172–173, 233
Butterfly bush, 167, 168, 169
Butterfly weed, 148, 149, 167, 176

C

Cabbage white butterfly, 173
Cactus, 158, 193
Campion, 111
Canada mayflower, 150, 151
Canadian wild rye, 155
Cardinal flower, 191
Cardinal, 181
Carrots, 45, 75, 90, 91, 216
Cedar waxwing, 181
Chickadee, 163, 180, 188
Chinese lantern, 112
Chipping sparrow, 181
Chives, 76, 77
Christmas fern, 150, 151
Chuparosa, 193
Claret cup cactus, 193
Clover, 123, 165
Columbine, 99, 193
Comma butterfly, 169

Community gardens, 223–225
Companion plants, 55
Compost:
    making, 15
    tea, 14, 71, 75, 117, 119, 120, 121
Composter, 14
Containers, 36–37
    bird gardens in, 187
    bulbs, 101
    butterfly gardens in, 175
    grasses in, 149
    hanging, 75, 105, 118–119
    herbs in, 77
    melons in, 66
    native plants in, 147
    in school gardens, 220
    strawberries in, 86
    tips for, 36, 37, 75
    tomatoes in, 68
    wildlife gardens in, 164
Coreopsis, 158, 167
Coriander, 70, 71, 216
Corn, 47, 60, 61, 62, 63, 90, 91, 218, 219
Cornflower, 95
Cosmos, 96, 167, 216
Cotton grass, 139
Crocus, 100
Cucumber, 46, 90, 91

D

Daffodil, 100, 101
Daisy, 106, 176, 194, 195
Dandelion, 34
Daphne, 108
Delphinium, 111, 125
Desert, 140, 144, 157, 158–159
Dill, 76, 77, 78, 167
Dogbane, 176
Dogwood, 143, 148, 149, 150, 151, 165, 182
Douglas fir, 142

E

Earthworms, 12, 13
Eastern black swallowtail butterfly, 173
Edge zone, 165
Elderberry, 194, 195, 199
Evening grosbeak, 182
Evening primrose, 108, 158

F

Fairy duster, 193
Fern, 150, 151, 202, 216
Feverfew, 109
Fireweed, 141
Flowering times, 22, 105
Flowering tobacco. *See* Nicotiana
Flowers:
　annuals, 94–96
　bulbs, 100–101
　containers for, 105, 118–119
　perennials, 97–99
　See also names of flowers
Foamflower, 99, 150, 151
Fountain grass, 115
Four o'clock, 111
Foxglove, 98, 99, 124
Fritillary, 109
Frost dates, 21
Fruit, 42, 66–67, 84–85, 86–87, 182, 196

G

Garden plan:
　bird habitat, 208
　bird thicket, 199
　bird's-eye view, 18–19
　butterfly, 167
　flower, 102–104
　grandma's, 125
　grassland, 148
　herb, 77
　hummingbird, 193
　monarch, 176
　native plants, 142, 148, 150, 155
　school, 206
　schoolyard peace, 215
　sweet-smelling, 108
　wildflower, 155
　wildlife, 165
　woodland, 150
　Victory Garden, 91
　xeriscape, 158
Garlic, 70, 71, 218
Gayfeather, 148
Geranium, 108, 150, 151, 216
Germination, 10
Globe thistle, 167, 199
Goldenrod, 34, 142, 148, 149, 155, 158,
　167, 176, 194, 195

Grass(es):
　big bluestem, 138, 148, 149
　Canadian wild rye, 155
　in containers, 149
　fountain, 115
　growing, 115, 144, 146, 148, 149
　Indian grass, 148, 149, 199
　switchgrass, 115, 149, 158, 165
　northern sea oats, 158
　native, 208
　in Special Needs Garden, 216
Grassland, 141, 144, 146, 148–149
Green onions, 44, 70, 71, 90, 91

H

Hardiness zones, 21, 22
Harvesting, 56, 59, 63, 70, 78
Hawthorn, 199, 208
Hemlock, 143, 150, 151
Hens and chickens, 114, 116, 221, 216
Herbicides, 35, 171
Herbs, 76–79
Hills, planting in , 49, 61–62, 64–65,
　66–67
Hollyhock, 125
Host plant, 111, 166, 170, 171, 172, 173,
　176, 177, 233
Hummingbirds, 190–193
Hyacinth, 100, 101, 105, 114

I

Indian grass, 148, 149, 199
Indian paintbrush, 148, 149
Insects:
　attracting, 184, 185, 196
　bad, 54, 184
　bees, 179
　as bird food, 184
　good, 55, 178, 184
　ladybugs, 178
　See also Butterflies
Inside-out flower, 142
Invasive plants, 129, 132, 145, 170
Ivy, 105, 145

J

Joe-Pye weed, 167, 176, 202
Jojoba, 193
Juniper, 199, 208

K

Karner blue butterfly, 171

L

Ladybug, 55, 178
Lamb's ears, 221, 216
Lavender, 108, 123, 125, 194, 195, 216
Lead plant, 148, 149
Lettuce, 44, 72, 73, 75, 90, 91
Lilac, 108, 125, 169
Lily, 111, 125, 133
Lily-of-the-valley, 99
Lobelia, 117
Lousewort, 133
Lupine, 158, 171

M

Madrone, 136
Marguerite, 117
Marigold, 71, 90, 91, 119, 122, 167
Marjoram, 77, 114
Mayflower, 150, 151
Melon, 66–67, 219
Milkweed, 167, 176–177, 191
Monarch butterfly, 172, 176–177
Money plant, 112
Monkey flower, 118, 119
Morning glory, 95
Mourning cloak butterfly, 172
Mulch, 13, 35, 52
Multicultural kitchen garden, 219

N

Narcissus. *See* Daffodil
Nasturtium, 73, 90, 91, 95, 119, 123, 216
Native plant(s):
　buying, 143
　communities, 140–141
　extinction of, 132–133
　garden plans, 142, 148, 150, 155
　grasses, 115, 148–149, 155, 157
　importance of, 130–131
　kinds of, 128–129
　planting, 146–147
　plant lists, 230–232
　regions, 134–135
　seed collecting, 152–153, 154–155
　wildflowers, 154–155, 215
　woodland, 150–151

238

Nectar, 169
Nests and nesting, 188, 189, 196, 197
New Jersey tea, 167
Nicotiana, 111, 216
Northern sea oats, 158

O

Obedient plant, 99
Ocotillo, 193
Old-fashioned plants, 109, 111, 120, 169
Oregano, 76, 77
Oregon grape, 142
Organic matter, 11, 12–13, 14

P

Painted lady butterfly, 170, 172
Pansy, 105, 117, 122
Parsley, 77, 90, 91, 167
Pasture rose, 148, 149
Peace garden, 214–215
Peas, 45, 75, 90, 91, 219
Penstemon, 193
Peony, 108
Peppers, 47, 70, 71, 90, 91, 218, 219
Perennials, 22, 97–99
Pesticides, 35, 171, 194
Pests, 54–55, 184, 200
Phlox, 108, 111, 167
Photosynthesis, 10
Pine, 165
Plan, garden. *See* Garden plan
Planning:
    bird's-eye view, 18–19
    flower gardens, 102–104
    schoolyard gardens, 206–207
Plant checklist:, 21
    flower, 102
    native plant, 143
    vegetable, 47
    wildlife garden, 163
Planting:
    containers, 36–37
    by the moon, 51
    raised beds, 49
    rows, 48
    seeds, 26, 27, 50, 154–155
    seedlings, 30–31
    squares, 49
    wide rows, 48

Plant(s):
    botanical name, 22
    choosing, 20–21
    edible, 40–43
    hardiness zone, 21
    labels, 22
    life cycle, 10
    native, 127–159, 230–232
    poisonous, 41, 88, 89
    shade-loving, 20, 41, 99
    for special needs gardens, 216
    sun-loving, 20
    types, 22
Pollination, 11, 179
Pollinators, 81, 108, 169, 179
Pond, toad, 202–203
Potatoes, 89, 90, 91
Pots. *See* Containers
Prickly pear cactus, 158
Pumpkin, 64–65, 90, 91, 218, 219
Purple coneflower, 97, 128, 155, 158, 183, 199
Purple finch, 181
Purple loosestrife, 129
Pussy toes, 221

Q

Queen Anne's lace, 129, 170, 178
Question mark butterfly, 173

R

Radish, 45, 75, 90, 91
Ragweed, 34, 142
Raised beds, 49, 217
Raspberry, 84–85
Red admiral butterfly, 172
Red cedar, 199
Red sage, 193
Rhododendron, 142
Rhubarb, 88
Rock cress, 116
Rocky Mountain penstemon, 137
Roses, 108, 120–121, 125, 148, 149, 191, 195, 199, 216
Rosemary, 76, 77, 108, 114
Row planting, 48, 86–87, 90–91
Ruby-throated hummingbird, 180, 192

S

Sage, 77, 193, 216
Saguaro cactus, 137
Salad vegetables, 72–73
Salal, 142
Salsa, 70–71
Sassafras, 139
Saw palmetto, 138
Saxifrage, 116
Scarecrow, 74–75
School gardens, 206–221
Sedge, 165, 202
Sedum, 116, 158, 167
Seedlings:
    buying, 30
    growing, 28–29
    planting, 30–31, 51
Seeds:
    chemical alert, 51
    growing, 28–29
    harvesting , 59
    native plant, 152–153
    saving, 58
    sowing, 26–27, 51
    wildflower, 152–153, 154–155
Serviceberry, 198, 199
Sexton Mountain mariposa lily, 133
Shade-loving plants, 20, 41, 99
Silver-spotted skipper butterfly, 173
Skunk cabbage, 109
Snapdragon, 96, 125, 167, 221
Soil:
    earthworms in, 12, 13
    mulching, 13
    organic matter, 13
    squeeze test, 26
Solomon's seal, 97, 99, 150, 151
Square planting, 49, 70–71, 90–91
Squash, 60, 61, 62, 63, 90, 91, 218
Statice, 112
Strawflower, 112, 113
Succession, 141
Sunflower, 82–83, 216, 218, 219
Sun-loving plants, 20
Sweet pea, 81
Sweet woodruff, 108, 216
Switchgrass, 115, 149, 158, 165

T

Thicket, bird, 198–199
Thistle, 112, 167, 170, 176, 191, 199
Thyme, 76, 77, 78, 79, 108, 114, 194, 195, 216
Tick trefoil, 155
Tiger swallowtail butterfly, 169
Toad garden, 200–203
Tomatoes, 46, 68–69, 70, 71, 75, 90, 91, 218, 219
Tools, garden, 24
Transplanting, 144
Trellises, 43, 68, 70, 71, 80–81, 90, 91, 217
Trillium, 99, 130, 150, 151
Trumpet vine, 191
Tulip, 100, 101, 216

V

Vegetables:
    cool-weather, 40
    feeding, 52
    harvesting, 56
    kinds of, 40–43
    mini, 74–75
    mulching, 52
    pest control, 54
    support for, 43, 68, 70, 71, 80–81, 90, 91, 217
    warm–weather, 42
    watering, 53
    weeding, 53
Verbena, 167
Viburnum, 150, 151, 216
Violet, 99, 108, 125
Virginia creeper, 199

W

Water lily, 202
Water:
    for birds, 186
    for butterflies, 175
    how to, 33
    rain barrel, 33
    rain gauge, 32
    soaker hose, 33
    saving, 156–157
    when to, 32

Weeds:
    common, 34
    good, 34, 171
    removing, 34
Western sword fern, 142
Wetland, 140, 202–203
White-fringed orchid, 132
Wild geranium, 150, 151
Wild ginger, 142
Wild grape, 165, 194, 195, 199
Wild rose, 120, 148, 149, 195, 199
Wild rye, 155
Wildflower(s):
    definition, 128
    garden, 154–155
    seeds, 152–153, 154
Wildlife:
    bird gardens, 180–199
    butterfly gardens, 166–177
    edge zone, 165
    garden plan, 165
    jigsaw garden, 228
    range, 163
    size, 164
    toad garden, 200–203
    See also Insects
Winterberry, 199
Wintergreen, 199
Witch hazel, 150, 151
Woodland, 140, 144, 146, 150–151
Wood sorrel, 142

X

Xeriscape, 156–157

Y

Yarrow, 98, 112, 194, 195
Yucca, 110, 111, 193

Z

Zinnia, 169
Zucchini, 90, 91, 219

Gardening Notes